D0804277

# Project Future

# Project Future

**THE INSIDE STORY BEHIND
THE CREATION OF DISNEY WORLD**

## Chad Denver Emerson

Ayefour Publishing

Copyright © 2010 by Chad Emerson

Cover and book design by Jennifer Solt.

All rights reserved.

No part of this book may be reproduced in any form or by any electronic or
mechanical means including information storage and retrieval systems, without
permission in writing from the author. The only exception is by a reviewer, who
may quote short excerpts in a review.

Visit us on-line at:
www.projectfuturebook.com
www.ayefourpublishing.com

Printed in the United States of America.

First Printing: 2010

ISBN-978-0-615-34777-6

To
Betsy and our boys, Owen, Dawson, and Cullen

# Contents

# Foreword

The Reedy Creek Improvement District has played an important role in the success of the Walt Disney World Resort. That much is very clear to everyone at Walt Disney World.

As Executive Vice President for Operations at Disney World, I often interacted with the leadership at Reedy Creek in a variety of ways. Their professional approach to governance, planning, public safety, and many other areas helped insure the success of Disney World since its earliest days.

We most appreciated Reedy Creek's excellence when there were medical emergencies involving guests or Cast Members. Their team always arrived on the scene very quickly and took the utmost professional care of every person. Personally, I most appreciated them when we had to open our Emergency Operations Center for events like 9/11 or hurricanes.

I was always relieved to see Mickey Shriver, Deputy District Administrator of Reedy Creek walk through the door of the emergency center to guide us through our preparations. He always stayed with us until every event was over and every guest and Cast Member was safe. Mickey was even nice to me when I complained that the traffic lights were too long or too short or that we needed a new street sign at some remote location.

From the beginning, Walt Disney World was an extremely unique project. It was a project that, in order to realize Walt's vision, required creative strategies aimed at providing an immersive experience for guests while allowing Disney to utilize innovative and sound regulatory and design strategies that were focused on safety and creativity.

To accomplish this, Walt and his team embraced a regulatory approach that would ultimately find near unanimous support from the Florida legislature, Governor's office, and local officials.  Until now, the story behind this groundbreaking effort has only been told in bits and pieces.

Chad Emerson's work in this book brings these events together into a complete story.  I've known Chad for several years as he was one of the first journalists to interview me after my retirement from Disney.  His focus on accurately telling interesting stories continues with this book.

"Project Future" does an excellent job providing rich details and historical context to the incredible efforts that individuals like Walt and Roy Disney, Bob Foster, Tom DeWolf, Paul Helliwell, Roy Hawkins and many others took to make Walt Disney World a reality.

If you are interested in understanding how the private Disney and public Reedy Creek worked together to create the world's most successful theme park resort, then "Project Future" provides a concise and interesting history of Disney World from the earliest days. It's a fun read that returns us all to the origins of Walt's Florida Project.

I hope that you, like me, enjoy this trip back to where the magic began.

—Lee Cockerell

# Acknowledgements

Writing this book was an amazing experience. Much of that has to do with the many interesting and helpful people that I met along the way.

Understanding how Disney World was created and how it operates required a great deal of guidance from others. I'm especially grateful to Lee Cockerell. I first met Lee while writing a feature on his career at Disney. He was gracious then and remains so now. Lee is truly one of the industry's great minds when it comes to promoting effective leadership.

In addition, I want to thank Brad Rex, Joni Newkirk, Greg Emmer and Steve Brown—all former Disney executives who shared their valuable time in reviewing sample chapters and providing feedback and encouragement.

And, while Disney did not provide any official assistance in developing this book, I would be remiss not to mention long-time Disney publicist Dave Herbst. During his tenure at Disney World, Dave has been highly respected by colleagues and the press alike. Working with him on various magazine articles has provided me with a better understanding of both Disney and the industry. Dave Herbst sets the bar when it comes to amusement industry publicity.

Located inside the official boundaries of the Walt Disney World Resort is the headquarters for the Reedy Creek Improvement District. Inside of that building is another great leader: Ray Maxwell, the long-time administrator for the District. Ray and his staff were incredibly helpful in providing information and responding to requests. Many Disney World guests may never realize it but their safety and fun has a great deal to do with the excellent work by Ray and his team.

I am also grateful for the Florida State University Law Review and its former Editor-in-Chief, Alyssa Lathrop. This book was in many ways born out of a law review article I published with FSU analyzing the Reedy Creek Improvement District. Alyssa and her faculty advisors, Professors Curtis Bridgeman and Robert Atkinson provided great support for that article and stood behind it through the entire process. I remain extremely grateful for that.

Thanks are also well-deserved for Dean Charles Nelson of Faulkner University's Thomas Goode Jones School of Law where I teach and my colleagues at the law school who have provided great support. A special thanks to Robb Farmer and Ned Swanner for helping me track down so many historical resources.

Part of the fun in writing this book was enjoying conversations with a wide variety of people involved in Project Future. These include Phil Smith, Tom DeWolf, Harrison "Buzz" Price, Governor Claude Kirk, and Robert Foster. These visionaries all played an important role in making Project Future a reality and I thank them for their time.

Taking all of these ideas and turning them into a book required a great deal of technical assistance. Thank you to Robyn Cannon for her excellent research help as well as Joy Bagley and Emily Marsh for their sharp eyes and bright ideas in editing and organizing the manuscript. I'm also very grateful for the publicity and marketing help that former Disney leader Vicki Johnson has provided. Vicki is one of the best connected and most resourceful publicity experts in the field.

Also, a big thank you goes to Jennifer Solt with 24 Communications. In addition to providing helpful feedback, she designed the cover and interior of the book. Project Future looks great because of Jennifer's fantastic design talent.

There are, of course, many others whose assistance made this book happen. The library teams at the University of Central Florida, the Orlando Public Library, and the Florida State Library all provided great support in finding the information to tell this story. The archivists at the Florida State Archives and the Southeast branch of the National Archives were also incredible resources. Thank you to all of them.

Finally, I am grateful to Scott Borowsky, Caroline Burns, and the team at Tourist Attractions and Parks Magazine where I write the Large Park Report column as well as Charlie Read and Judy Rubin at BlooLoop.com where I serve as a contributor. Both of these publications have provided me with the means for meeting many of the people who helped tell this story. I am fortunate to have such fantastic colleagues.

Because this is a book about Disney, in closing, I have one "wish" that I would like to make. The team at Disney's private archives in Burbank, California is brilliant in many ways. However, I hope that they would consider re-opening those archives to researchers. They were once open but now have been essentially closed to almost all projects. That is a shame because in those archives reside a wealth of knowledge on the history of Disney. At the very least, please consider establishing a formal process by which researchers can propose use of the Disney archives.

I hope that you enjoy this book. It was a great adventure to research and write. I have purposefully kept it at a manageable length without sacrificing important details. My goal was to create an interesting book that would, whether relaxing on the beach, flying in a plane to Disney World, or anywhere else, provide the reader with a look at how the magic of the Walt Disney World Resort came to be.

—Chad Emerson

# Introduction

On November 22, 1963, one airplane flight changed not only the future of Central Florida but also that of the entire nation. Aboard the plane was Walter "Walt" Elias Disney, the creative genius who ushered in a new era of American entertainment through his animated feature films and Disneyland theme park in Anaheim, California. From his window seat, he looked down on thousands of acres of rural swampland and orange groves, an environment that hardly seemed ripe for what would become one of the largest private developments ever in the United States. Yet, with his foresight, he saw an opportunity where other people did not, so much so that a small team of Disney confidants soon began acquiring twenty-seven thousand of those isolated acres for what would become the iconic Walt Disney World Resort. Even before that plane flight, Walt's interest in creating an eastern project to accompany his Disneyland park in California had been piqued.

This story recounts the amazing set of events that enabled Walt Disney's vision to become a reality.

From obscure legal strategies to spy-like maneuvers, Disney's eastern plans, code named Project Future, were built upon a brilliant mix of fantasy and reality. The complexity of the final result, the Walt Disney World Resort, was rivaled only by the complexity of the method used to achieve it. Throughout the entire effort, two restrictions repeated themselves at almost every stage: Disney's insistence on secrecy in the process and Disney's desire for control of the product. This is not to say Disney had any nefarious intentions with these goals. Instead, the commitment to secrecy and control were natural extensions of frustrations Disney had encountered in previous creative projects.

Project Future would be Disney's most daunting challenge yet. For the grand vision to succeed, Disney examined lessons learned from the past and committed to avoiding them in the future. In the end, Disney's quest for a Florida project would be built less on pixie dust than on a determined, clever effort to turn an isolated piece of Central Florida into one of the world's leading tourist destinations.

This is the story of how Project Future forever changed the American amusement industry.

Chapter 1 1959-1963

# The Eastward Search Begins

With high expectations, on July 17, 1955, in Anaheim, California, Walt Disney officially opened Disneyland, a new type of amusement park that promised a family-friendly form of entertainment different from the notorious midways of the era. Media, dignitaries, and leaders from around the world gathered in Anaheim for the debut. The buzz was palpable. Disney, the inspired creator of fantasy through film, was now bringing fantasy to life.

Despite a host of operational challenges in Disneyland's early days, the park quickly became a major success. It was the culmination of Walt's innovative vision of a place where the family could ride rides together in a safe and clean setting, a place the entire family could enjoy together—an idea that had lingered in Walt's mind for several years.

Two years earlier, Walt had approached several close friends who were architects to get their input on how a Disney amusement park might be uniquely created. He wanted to use the latest in design and construction techniques to bring his vision into reality. At the same time, he knew such a venture would have to make business sense, so he commissioned feasibility and site studies for the proposed project. Fortunately, the studies revealed that a market did exist for his new type of family-oriented amusement venture.

With Disneyland a hit on the west coast, exporting Walt's unique brand of recreation to the east coast made perfect sense. The idea of building an east coast project was also based on practical concerns. Disney had hired a large stable of creative talent to develop and to open Disneyland. Now that it was open, the company could hire some of that talent to continue to work on new projects for the park. However, expansion at Disneyland alone would not support Walt's growing interest in amusement attractions nor would it provide enough work to keep all of these workers employed.

Even with Disneyland's early success, the company was searching for other ways to defray the costs needed to develop the new technologies that would enable Walt's visionary ideas, an especially urgent need since the possibility of building a Disney project on the east coast seemed likely. Somehow Disney had to find a way to reduce expenses without reducing creativity. The 1964-65 World's Fair in New York City offered the perfect interim step. Walt could develop attractions for the fair and test whether his type of entertainment would work with eastern U.S. audiences, a large group that so far comprised only a small part of Disneyland's attendance.

Ultimately, Disney's creative arm, WED Enterprises, entered into agreements with General Electric, Ford Motor Company, PepsiCo, and the State of Illinois, Walt's birthplace, to develop attractions for the fair. Yet by its very nature, a World's Fair is a temporary effort with a distinct beginning and ending date. If Walt wanted a continuing presence in the eastern part of the United States, he would need a permanent project.

With Disneyland's success increasing every year, Disney found itself with many suitors for another amusement park. In fact, within a year of Disneyland's 1955 opening, the company received numerous letters from individuals throughout the eastern U.S. proposing expansion into their city or state. Almost all of the letters received a polite response that Disney was not interested. Every now and then, though, one of the ideas would pique Walt's interest.

## Searching Outside of Florida

One of the earliest sites to do so was located near New York City in an area known as the New Jersey Meadows. According to an interview that Roy O. Disney, Walt's older brother and the person in charge of the company's business operations, gave to a local newspaper at the time, "Walt gave the Meadows proposal a careful look, but he finally decided that there would have to be some method for controlling the weather—a vast dome or some such thing. When the financial backers looked into the cost of such an undertaking, they lost their courage pretty fast."

## Niagara Falls

Another proposal came from Seagram's, the well-known liquor company. The idea involved a Disney role in developing tourist attractions at Niagara Falls. The irony of the proposal was that Walt himself had almost completely banned the sale of alcohol at Disneyland. Nevertheless, his interest in an attraction at Niagara Falls was serious enough that he visited the Falls in August of 1963 and met with local officials about the potential project. Traveling on a Beechcraft plane the company had recently purchased, Walt arrived in Niagara with his wife, Lillian; his brother, Roy; and Roy's wife, Edna.

They checked into the Hotel Sheraton Brock and that evening joined city officials for dinner at the home of a local business leader, Paul Schoellkopf. The next morning, Walt met with Franklin Miller, Mayor of Niagara Falls, and received a bird's-eye tour of the Falls from an observation tower. At the top, autograph-seeking fans surrounded Walt, and he obliged many of them before being whisked off to an elevator for the trip back down. The excitement surrounding Walt's visit was so intense though that a woman squeezed into the elevator to meet him, leaving her husband and children alone at the top of the tower. The behavior more typically experienced by a rock star or movie icon was now being shown to Walt.

While he denied considering a second Disneyland in Niagara, Walt did confirm he was negotiating to participate in another type of project on the Canadian side of the Falls. He would not give any more details, but news reports linked his interest to an expansion of the Seagram Tower, a local attraction which opened in June 1962 as the brainchild of several area business leaders headed by C. H. Augspurger from Buffalo, New York.

Designed by the Canadian architecture firm of Horton and Bell, the tower was located on a nearly two-acre parcel overlooking Niagara's Horseshoe Falls. It was there that the parties discussed Disney's involvement in developing a "moon trip" attraction on the tower site. However, despite these meetings, the Niagara plans never materialized.

Though the Niagara idea was shelved, another proposal from 1963 did proceed well beyond the discussion stage—a waterfront amusement facility in St. Louis. Unlike Disneyland and its original sixty-five-plus acres, the St. Louis project was to be built on only two and a half acres. To compensate for this small footprint, the project would grow vertically in a five-story structure.

The idea of a Disney project in St. Louis made a great deal of sense. Some of Walt's most formative years were spent in Missouri. Born in Illinois, he was raised in Marceline, Missouri, a small town that inspired Disneyland's Main Street. In addition to Marceline, Disney spent part of his childhood attending elementary school in Kansas City, Missouri. Then, after spending his teenage years in Chicago, he returned to Kansas City and began his earliest work in the world of art and drawing. All in all, his deep roots in the Missouri area gave the state a head start for potential future projects.

### Signboard Hill, Kansas City, Missouri

Even before the St. Louis proposal, J.C. Hall, Walt's friend who founded the Hallmark greeting card company, recruited Disney to participate in a one hundred-plus acre project that would revolve around Walt's love of nature and would include an international-themed village—a concept that would eventually make its way into the Disney sphere as World Showcase at the EPCOT theme park. To be located in a somewhat blighted area of Kansas City known as Signboard Hill, the project would also house Hallmark's new headquarters known as the Crown Center.

Because Walt spent some of his most important years in Kansas City, the idea of working in the area must have been not only intriguing but also must have lent a sense of familiarity to the proposed project. He was interested enough that he signed on as a consultant and gave Hall a key piece of advice based on his Disneyland experience: buy enough land to create a strong buffer between the Hallmark property and surrounding landowners. This was a lesson Walt learned when, after Disneyland's opening, all types of motels, shopping facilities, and restaurants popped up around his park. Worse, the vast majority of those businesses did not embrace Walt's high design and visual appeal standards.

Even though Walt ultimately opted not to participate in the Signboard Hill project, his advice to Hill would later play a significant role in the planning of Project Future.

## Marceline, Missouri

Another Missouri location Walt considered was in the small town of Marceline where he lived until age nine. Initially the project itself was slated for a forty-five-acre farm his parents had purchased in the early 1900s. Although he lived in Marceline for only five years, both the town and the farm had lasting impacts on his creative life. For example, the small Marceline main street inspired Disneyland's Main Street USA. Walt also built a replica of the farm's red barn in his backyard in Los Angeles.

It was hardly surprising, then, when in the 1940s Walt began to dream about a project of some type in Marceline. By 1956 the dream had developed into a concrete idea. During a visit to Marceline that year, Walt stayed at the home of local businessman Rush Johnson, in part because it was one of the few air-conditioned homes in the still small Marceline. Johnson and Walt developed a close relationship most likely because both shared a visionary type of entrepreneurship.

The plans for a Marceline project were crafted one evening as they stayed up late. Walt explained his idea of opening an attraction on the old family farm in Marceline. As a big booster of Marceline, the civic-oriented Johnson quickly moved on the idea.

A key strategy for the project would end up foreshadowing Disney's later efforts in Florida. In particular, Walt insisted on obtaining the old farm and surrounding land without using his name. He was concerned the use of his name would result in increased prices through land speculation. This very concern would manifest itself several years later as he acquired acreage in Central Florida using dummy corporations whose names were not tied to Disney. To do this, Johnson established a nonprofit corporation for purchasing land for the Marceline project. Once it acquired all of the land, the corporation would then sell the land to Disney's company.

The project itself would have featured a turn-of-the-century working farm that doubled as a tourist attraction. Obviously, a project in the hometown of Walt's childhood would appeal to many people. Walt's interest was strong enough that in 1965 he hired Harrison "Buzz" Price and his firm, Economic Research Associates [ERA], to conduct a feasibility analysis, one of more than a hundred studies ERA conducted for various Disney projects. Price was no stranger to Walt as he had conducted feasibility studies for Disneyland while working at the Stanford Research Institute. Unlike the studies for Disneyland though, the report on the Marceline project showed it was not likely to be profitable. Rather than be deterred, Walt proceeded under a not-for-profit scenario.

Rush Johnson traveled to Disney's Burbank office several times over the next decade to discuss the plans, and Disney even developed blueprints for the site. However, after Walt's death in 1966, the Marceline effort lost its priority in the company. Although Roy Disney kept the project alive for a time, company officials abandoned plans for the project several years following Walt's death. In the end, Johnson repurchased the land and later gave it to his daughter as a wedding gift.

## The St. Louis Waterfront

The St. Louis project came even closer to being built than the Marceline project. Disney's strong ties to Missouri undoubtedly again played a significant role. In March 1963 St. Louis officials called Disney about plans to revitalize the city's waterfront, an effort that would include building a new baseball stadium downtown for the St. Louis Cardinals and constructing the iconic Gateway Arch. Initially though, city officials were not aiming for a Disney amusement project. Instead, they simply asked Walt to develop a film that would help celebrate the city's 200th anniversary in 1964.

Disney was interested but suggested that they all think in bigger terms. Instead of only a film, he thought the parties should discuss the possibility of an entertainment project. The idea intrigued city officials so much that, in March 1963, Mayor Raymond Tucker and a delegation of business leaders traveled to Disney's Burbank headquarters to discuss the project in more detail. Participants in the meeting also included Raymond Wittcoff, president of the Downtown Redevelopment Corporation, and leaders of the Civic Center Redevelopment Corporation who were charged with coordinating the waterfront project.

The meeting seemed to go well. Mayor Tucker reported that Walt himself was "personally interested" in the project. The delegation toured Disneyland and spent several hours with Walt discussing the plans. Not only would the project connect him to his Missouri roots but St. Louis's location near the new interstate highway system would also be an advantage.

In mid-April 1963, Disney dispatched company executive Donn Tatum to St. Louis to tour the prospective project site. Buzz Price, whose firm would again be hired to conduct the feasibility study, accompanied Tatum. The trip generated enough interest that in May 1963 Walt himself traveled to St. Louis with his wife, Lillian; daughter, Sharon; and son-in-law, Robert Brown, an architect from Kansas City. Wittcoff and other city leaders took Walt on a tour of the riverfront area and also showed him the view of the site from the rooftops of several of St. Louis's tallest buildings.

During this visit, Disney suggested that, considering St. Louis's cold winters, a year-round, indoor amusement facility on the 160,000 square-foot site might be the best option. He cautiously noted, though, that many of his creative leaders were in the throes of planning for the upcoming New York World's Fair and that ERA had only just begun its feasibility study. Both of these situations would delay an immediate commitment. Thus, without agreeing to anything, Disney and his family left St. Louis. When ERA, operating under the name Riverfront Square, released its report in August 1963, it concluded the project was feasible, resulting in Walt's return in November 1963.

While the parties began planning details in earnest, the first public misstep for the project occurred. During a news conference, Walt said liquor could not be served on the project's site if he were involved in it. This should have not been a surprise to anyone. After all, to promote a family atmosphere at Disneyland, Walt had prohibited alcohol sales in the public areas of the park. St. Louis differed from Anaheim, though, especially considering St. Louis was the home of the Anheuser-Busch beer company. To Walt's refusal, the St. Louis Post-Dispatch reported that Preston Estep, one of the project's chief backers, responded:

Any plans developed either by Mr. Disney or anyone else would not be approved if they did not provide for the sale of beer, wine and liquor in the restaurants and other appropriate entertainment facilities in the area.

The disagreement escalated at a dinner party the Disney group attended in St. Louis. It was there that August Busch Jr. loudly proclaimed Walt's no-alcohol idea was foolish. This offended Walt. After all, he was the creator of the wildly successful Disneyland. He was an expert at knowing what people did and did not want when visiting an amusement attraction. Why did these St. Louis officials think they knew more than him?

Soon Disney's colleagues realized the alcohol issue would end up being a major hurdle for Riverfront Square. Apparently, though, the issue alone was not enough to derail the project. That was left to another problem.

Walt had told St. Louis officials that he would have to be the sole builder and operator of the amusement facility. "We've got to be responsible for the whole thing if it's got the Disney name connected with it," he explained. After his Disneyland experience, Disney's insistence on control became a common demand, one that would play a major role in the Florida project. Yet at the time, even with this mandate, St. Louis and Disney agreed to move forward with the project.

By 1964 the New York Times was reporting that the project was scheduled for completion in 1966 or 1967, a strong indication the proposal had advanced beyond the idea stage. General William "Joe" Potter, the retired military officer whom Disney later hired to lead the development of his Florida project, supported this notion. In his military memoir, he explained:

> Ever since Disneyland was a success he'd been importuned by other states and by foreign nations to build other Disneylands. We almost built one in St. Louis... Designs were well under way. It was going to be in a high-rise rather than in a ground-level place.

In March 1964, Walt returned to St. Louis and attended a press conference at the Bel-Air East Motel. During this meeting, he described his vision for the St. Louis project, which would be located next to the new downtown baseball stadium. The parties had agreed that alcohol would be available in designated areas only. The project would be built in a multi-story building, which would include at least one floor below ground. At the subterranean level, guests would discover a blue-bayou boat ride and a pirates' lair. On the ground level they would discover a town square which Disney promotional materials described as follows:

> On one side would be Old St. Louis and on the other Old New Orleans, with a pre-Civil War haunted house nearby. Elsewhere there would be theaters with depictions of the Lewis and Clark expedition, the Louisiana Purchase and other historical events.

A major component of the town square would be cutting-edge light technology that allowed the area to change from morning to night over the course of the day. The two upper levels would be for dining, offices, and banquet space. All in all, the project was filled with ideas from existing or upcoming Disney attractions such as the Haunted Mansion and Pirates of the Caribbean. Disney estimated four hours on site would be necessary to experience the entire project.

Indicating seriousness in the project, Walt assigned Marvin Davis, one of his most trusted designers, to work on plans for the project. Davis had worked closely with Disney in bringing Disneyland into reality. However, excitement about the St. Louis project was short-lived.

During the next year, the project came to a halt, the biggest problem apparently being finances. Although Walt insisted on owning the project if it were going to include the Disney name, the company did not want to financially invest in the project beyond offering design and operational services. Walt expected the city to pay for construction and to reimburse him for operating costs. The city countered that, if Walt owned the project, he should pay for its construction, albeit with some financial incentives. What the city did not realize was that Disney was, at the same time, committing millions of dollars to purchase land in Central Florida. Simultaneously investing large amounts of money into the Riverfront project would be difficult.

By June of 1965, parties were describing the project as "neither dead nor too alive." In reality, the prospects had become so bleak that city officials leased the proposed site to a surface parking lot company. However, in a final effort to salvage the project, St. Louis officials traveled to Burbank in July 1965. There, the parties discussed the project's potential $30 to $50 million price tag and whether the proposed facility was large enough to accommodate the twenty-five thousand daily guests needed to make the project work.

Reports following the Burbank meeting indicated the project was likely dead. These were confirmed several days later when a delegation of Disney executives, led by Roy Disney, traveled back to the Bel-Air East Motel for a private meeting with St. Louis officials. Following the meeting, the St. Louis Post-Dispatch reported on a statement released to the local press:

> *We were asked to try to develop a major*
> *attraction having the impact on the St.*

*Louis area of a Disneyland. We suggested
at the outset that a project of that scope, in
size and cost, might well prove difficult to
accomplish, due to a number of imponderable
factors. Such has proved to be the case.*

With that, a midwestern Disneyland in Walt's beloved
Missouri was finished before it ever began. Little did the
world know though Disney's search for a sequel project
was actually picking up steam nearly one thousand miles to
the southeast of St. Louis.

A major problem with the proposed New Jersey,
Niagara, and St. Louis projects was that winter weather
would have required indoor facilities, translating into
increased building and engineering costs. An indoor setting
would also limit the height and size of the potential rides
and attractions. Although these factors were not fatal flaws,
they certainly did not make things easier. In order to get
around the challenges of cold weather, Disney seemed to
grow more interested in the southeastern United States as
the best option for his second amusement resort.

The conventional wisdom of the time was that amusement
parks were primarily for the summer season. Disneyland's
location in the warm climate of southern California had
countered that theory by showing that a market existed for
year-round park visitors. This fact led Walt to narrow down
his strongest interest in an eastern project to South Carolina,
Georgia, Alabama, and Florida, all of them offering weather
usually warm enough for operating an outdoor theme park

year round, especially in the southernmost parts of those states. Among these options, Walt kept coming back to the Sunshine State as the most likely location for his second major amusement project.

## Searching Florida, 1959-1960

As in Missouri, Walt had several connections to Florida. In the late 1800s, his father, Elias, had moved to the state. There he met and married Flora Call, Disney's mother, and some time later purchased an orange grove. Walt's oldest sibling, Herbert, was also born in Florida. Later Elias Disney moved his family to Chicago where Walt and his younger sister, Ruth, were born. Walt's return to Florida would bring his family's history full circle.

### Palm Beach

One of the earliest indications of Walt's interest in Florida occurred at a June 1959 meeting during in Burbank, California, with NBC executives.   The executives had scheduled the meeting hoping to persuade Walt to partner with NBC in developing a theme park in New York. The network's interest in working with Walt resulted from the fact that he might be moving his weekly television show from ABC to NBC. The idea of tying his show with a theme-park project was not unprecedented. Indeed, ABC had been one of Disneyland's early investors as part of a sponsorship agreement that included airing the Disney show.

For the New York proposal, Disney hired Buzz Price's ERA to conduct a market analysis and NBC hired Price's former employer, the Stanford Research Institute, to do a similar study.

Ultimately, Walt declined to participate in the New York theme-park project because of concerns about a short operating season and the cost of acquiring land in the area. Yet his decline did not represent the end of his work with NBC. That same year, he and NBC discussed developing a project in the Palm Beach, Florida area on land owned by John D. MacArthur, an eccentric billionaire who had made much of his money by starting the Bankers Life and Casualty Company. With this wealth, MacArthur had purchased huge tracts of land in North Palm Beach County.

Disney's specific interest in a Florida resort became particularly focused when Buzz Price conducted two Florida-based studies in 1959, one related to the recreation market in Florida and another related to the feasibility of developing a Disney resort in Palm Beach. The original Palm Beach proposal involved a venture between Disney, MacArthur, and the Radio Corporation of America [RCA], at the time owned by NBC. Walt conceived of more than just a version of Disneyland on the east coast. Instead, building on his growing interest in cities and urban development, the Palm Beach project called for a "Community of Tomorrow," which included a four-hundred-acre theme park and a town center for seventy thousand people.

Walt's interest was so serious that he assigned Marvin Davis to prepare renderings and concept drawings. The project served as one of the earliest incarnations of Disney's

Experimental Prototype Community of Tomorrow, or EPCOT.

To get started on the study, Buzz Price flew to Palm Beach in the winter of 1959, toured twelve thousand acres on the city's north side, and began compiling information about the area and site. Following the trip, he prepared a report dated December 14, 1959, entitled "The Economic Setting of the City of Tomorrow."

The prospects seemed encouraging so Walt traveled to South Florida and met with MacArthur. Checking into the Palm Beach Towers for a week-long stay, Walt used a fictitious name to avoid publicity. This move was the first of many the company would take over the next decade to keep its interest in Florida secret.

Disney and MacArthur became fast friends as they toured the area in MacArthur's classic, large-finned Cadillac. They focused on a modest-sized parcel of several hundred acres, much less than seemed necessary to avoid neighboring landowners encroaching on the resort as they did at Disneyland. Nevertheless, Disney and MacArthur shook hands in agreement on the land deal.

In early 1960, Price returned to Palm Beach and met with the three prospective developers of the project, but a problem arose subsequently when Roy Disney visited and began finalizing the terms of the deal. Roy had traveled to Palm Beach to discuss the project with MacArthur's people. During the meeting, he pressed the need for more property. He did not want to relive the problem faced in Anaheim. MacArthur was offended, though. He perceived Roy Disney's request as an attempt to renegotiate Walt's agreement, and he left before completing negotiations.

"I have to get the hell out of here or I'll hit that goddamn beagle right in the nose," MacArthur said of Roy according to a subsequent article in the Palm Beach Post.

Later one of MacArthur's close colleagues claimed that Roy Disney's request for more property played a key role in the project's demise. Ultimately, though, the project failed because RCA balked at the cost. That and the fact that Disney's other projects were consuming a large amount of time led the parties to table the City of Tomorrow proposal.

## Ocala, Florida

Even with this setback, Walt remained interested in developing a project in Florida. Not long after, he hired ERA to conduct preliminary research into the Tampa-St. Petersburg region. Even though the Tampa idea never developed beyond the discussion stage, in 1961 the company retained ERA to "explore the rural and vacation markets in Florida and to evaluate specific locations for future recreation facilities." For this study, Price hired freelance researcher Robert Lorimer to gather tourist data from throughout the state.

Lorimer traveled to Florida for a two-week "field trip" during which time he researched nearly every region of the Sunshine State to determine key factors such as weather, infrastructure, and vacation trends. He also visited several attractions in the state, including Marineland and Seaquarium.

Lorimer's report suggested Ocala as the prime site for a Florida project. Unfortunately, Lorimer missed the fact that highway plans called for both the Florida Turnpike and Interstate 4 to intersect near Orlando rather than Ocala, making Lorimer's recommendation based on bad information.

During this time, rumors of a potential Disneyland park in Florida began to spread throughout the Florida business community. Many of the rumors had to do with the efforts of Florida Governor Cecil Farris Bryant to recruit Disney. The near miss in Palm Beach had whetted the state's appetite for attracting some version of an eastern Disneyland to the Sunshine State.

In January 1962 prospects looked good. So much so that Percy Hopkins, mayor of West Palm Beach, and Bud Dickinson, a key business leader in Florida, requested a meeting with Governor C. Farris Bryant "concerning the establishment of a Disneyland in the State of Florida." Though that 1962 meeting was cancelled, Walt's plans for a Florida resort continued in earnest. Indeed, a major move was on the horizon.

Chapter 2 1963-1964

# The Search Is Completed

---

Almost every American vacationer recognizes Walt Disney World as one of the country's most popular tourist destinations. Yet this well-known Orlando-area destination has not always been known by that famous moniker. Before it was Disney World, the project's name alternated among a series of code word titles. For instance, in 1964 it was known as Project Winter, the counterpart for a series of other seasonally-coded Disney proposals known as Project Fall, the St. Louis project; Project Summer, the Niagara proposal; and Project Spring, a proposed joint venture near Monterey, California, between Walt Disney and Samuel Morse, who headed the Del Monte properties and owned the Pebble Beach Resort in Monterey County. The Monterey proposal had generated enough interest that Disney commissioned two studies in 1963 to explore its potential. Eventually, though, the company decided not to proceed.

These seasonal projects were part of a wave of proposed Disney projects during the 1960s. The State of Florida, from the beginning though, was the most likely place to expand the Disney amusement-park enterprise. At times the proposed Florida resort was referred to as Project Florida, Project X, and Disneyland-East, but in June 1965 Disney officials settled on Project Future. In November of that same year, the company officially announced the project as Disneyworld, a name Roy Disney changed to the current Walt Disney World Resort after his brother's death in December 1966.

Another Disney plane tour of the eastern United States, during which Central Florida gained momentum as the choice location, preceded all of this name changing. On Sunday, November 17, 1963, Buzz Price joined Walt and other company officials, including Disney vice presidents Joe Fowler, Donn Tatum, Jack Sayers, and Esmond Cardon "Card" Walker, some of Disney's brightest minds, for the trip. Fowler had played a key role in the construction of Disneyland, and Walker had worked his way up from an entry-level position in the mailroom to an executive role. Like Walker, Tatum, a close confidant of Roy Disney, would later serve a stint as the company's CEO and Chairman. Tatum also had the distinction of being the first non-Disney family member to hold the position of president in the company. All in all, the delegation on the plane represented many of the key figures involved in bringing the Florida project to fruition.

The group was originally scheduled to leave on a Grumman turboprop that Disney had ordered for company use, but the plane was not ready in time for the trip. As a result, Grumman furnished a loaner plane, the same model but without exterior markings to indicate a Disney team was on board. Though not intentional, this anonymity served Walt's purpose of keeping a low, if not entirely secret, profile.

At the time of the trip, Walt was considering numerous proposals across the country for developing entertainment and amusement attractions. These considerations were in addition to the continued growth of Disneyland and Disney's involvement in the New York World's Fair. A consensus was growing in the company though that it was time to either move forward or to reject the various proposals. Too much time was being spent on the possible rather than the actual. Disney needed to make a decision on whether it would develop a project on the east coast and, if so, where.

The November 1963 plane tour was supposed to move this process along. The trip began with stops in St. Louis, Niagara Falls, and the Washington D.C. area where the Disney entourage toured potential sites for a Disney project in those areas.

## Ocala, Florida, Revisited

Then, on Thursday of that week, the group landed at Orlando's Executive Airport, then known as Herndon Airport. Upon landing, the Disney team, in two rental cars, headed toward Ocala. Walt was riding with Buzz Price when the group passed the Citrus Tower in Clermont, Florida which, at the time, was one of the few tourist attractions in the area.

Upon arriving in Ocala, the group checked into a local hotel. To keep a low profile, Walt did not register using his famous name. Instead, he reserved his room under the fictional name William Brown. Even so, several people, including the waitress at dinner, recognized him and asked for his autograph. Walt graciously agreed—and signed the name William Brown.

The next morning, Friday, November 22, the group returned to Orlando for the flight back to California. Walt instructed the pilots to fly over various Floridian locations, including Central Florida. They flew south to the Florida Keys, northwest to Ft. Myers, and north up the west coast to St. Petersburg and Tampa. The low-altitude tour gave Disney and his companions a bird's-eye view of the east, south, and west coasts of Florida.

Last, they flew over the Gulf of Mexico toward New Orleans, arriving in the Big Easy about 6:30 p.m. Upon landing, they learned President John F. Kennedy had been assassinated earlier that day. On the somber final leg back to

California, Walt announced to those on board that Central Florida appeared to be the choice location.

Soon after landing in California, Walt asked Buzz Price to begin researching prospective properties in Central Florida. The following week, ERA submitted Proposal No. 1021 to Disney for a detailed study of Florida sites. The November 1963 proposal was quickly approved, and Price assigned responsibility for "Project 395" to William Lund. Like Price himself, Lund had previously worked with the Stanford Research Institute. He was also somewhat familiar with Central Florida, for he had traveled to the Tampa area with another Disney official, Robert Gurr, in October of that year to attend a conference that examined the use of automated people movers at airports in the United States. The movers were similar to those the company operated in Disneyland.

On November 27, 1963, Lund and Price joined Walt and Roy Disney, Walker, Tatum, and Fowler for a follow-up meeting about the recent plane trip. Other Disney officials at the meeting included company attorney Robert Foster, General Counsel Dick Morrow, company treasurers Larry Tryon and O.V. Melton, and a company vice president, Jack Sayers. Even more than the previous week's plane trip, this meeting included the hierarchy of Disney leadership. The day's topic clearly warranted as much.

The group gathered in Conference Room 2E, a mahogany-lined room often used for important meetings at the Walt Disney headquarters. Some of the company's most critical decisions were often discussed in this room. To get started,

Price distributed copies of the proposal to develop a resort in Florida. Much of the discussion centered on identifying potential parcels that would be large enough for the project. Although the mood seemed encouraging, Walt did not formally approve the ERA proposal at the meeting. Instead, with Thanksgiving the next day, he decided to think it over. As the meeting concluded, Price gathered up the copies of the proposal he had circulated at the meeting, and the Disney officials instructed him to guard the copies closely. They wanted to be sure the information did not leak outside of their small working group.

The day after Thanksgiving, Price and Lund returned to the Disney offices and met with Disney executives Card Walker and Donn Tatum. During the meeting, they gave ERA the go-ahead to proceed with plans for what would now be referred to as Project Winter, an effort for which ERA would be paid $4,900 to survey the state of Florida and to examine its prospects for a Disney development. They also told Lund, who would be traveling to Florida, that he should not identify himself with either Disney or ERA during his research. Instead, he would simply tell anyone that asked that he was advising a client on investment in Florida real estate. Once again, secrecy was the key.

Disney further disguised Lund's identity when Dick Morrow reached out to company's New York-based legal counsel, Donovan, Leisure, Newton & Irvine, for an important favor. Morrow's request was simple. Could the firm arrange the printing of business cards for Lund identifying him as an attorney with Burke & Burke, a law firm with main offices one floor below those of the Donovan firm?

The New York attorneys agreed and, in addition to the business cards, arranged to have all Florida-related phone calls and correspondence to Lund routed through Burke's office at One Wall Street in Manhattan. Under that arrangement, upon receiving a call or letter to Lund, someone at Burke would notify Lund in California. The system further insulated Lund, ERA, and Disney from direct contact between California and Florida and by doing so, limited the possibility of an inadvertent disclosure of Disney's identity.

On December 9, 1963, Lund flew from California to Tampa, rented a car, and drove to Orlando to begin research for Project Future. He checked into the Robert Meyer Hotel, an establishment that, as the story unfolds, would become a familiar place to Disney officials.

After arriving, he called bank executives at the Florida National Bank and First National Bank of Florida and asked for recommendations about local real estate experts. Obliging bank executives suggested contacting either Florida Ranch Lands [FRL] or the Brass and Hainey firm.

Lund first toured the Orlando area himself and then called FRL. He spoke with David Nusbickel, who invited Lund to his real estate office that afternoon. Lund gave Nusbickel the Burke & Burke business card and explained that his confidential client was interested in large tracts of land in Florida. Nusbickel indicated that his firm had experience in that area, and he and Lund agreed to meet again the next day. The air of mystery gave Nusbickel some pause, though, and he asked his firm's counsel to investigate Lund's Burke & Burke story. The attorney reported back that the Burke firm was legit; he had not discovered though that Lund was not actually a lawyer with Burke & Burke. For now the secret remained secure.

The next morning Lund met with T.R. McElwee at Brass and Hainey, and McElwee gave Lund a general tour of the area. Later that same week FRL's Nusbickel gave Lund a short private plane ride around the area. Lund spent his third day in Orlando visiting the Chamber of Commerce and government entities such as utilities and transportation departments and the planning commission, all to get information about current and potential development in Florida. The next day Lund drove to Ocala and conducted similar research into whether that area was a viable option for the Disney project. Then, having completed the research in Central Florida, he traveled to the Miami area to investigate prospects in South Florida and finally made a quick visit to Jacksonville before returning home to California.

A primary objective of Lund's efforts was "to evaluate in greater detail the location advantages offered by Ocala versus Orlando." The consideration of these locations had started two years earlier with the 1961 ERA report that indicated "the Ocala area was the optimum geographic location for such a project because of the large number of out-of-state visitors . . . that passed through or near the city annually." Since that time, two major highways, I-4 between Orlando and Tampa and the extension of the Florida Turnpike to Orlando, were nearing completion. Orlando's drive-through exposure would compete with, if not exceed, that of Ocala.

Upon returning to California, Lund briefed Price on his findings and fielded a call from Nusbickel, who informed Lund that one of the Central Florida parcels they toured was under contract. As it turned out, this parcel was the same that would end up composing a major portion of Project Future. But at the time, few, if any, at Disney even knew that property existed.

After briefing Price, Lund prepared a report chronicling the results of his research and during the second week in January they again joined the small Disney working group in Conference Room 2E and presented the report. Entitled "Preliminary Investigation of Available Acreage for Project Winter," it focused attention on the Orlando area. The report concluded Orlando "offers greater potential for the development of Project Winter than does the Ocala area" since "Orlando has a large, growing, and healthy economic base to help sustain" a project of this magnitude.

Still, the idea of operating a year-round theme-park resort in Central Florida was not without concerns. Issues such as the area's insect problems, hurricane threats, regular thunderstorms, and climate—periodic cold winter days and a consistently hot, humid summer season—meant the area compared much less favorably to the more temperate conditions at Disneyland in southern California. Yet Walt seemed undeterred and remained convinced that Central Florida was the best option for his next resort destination.

With the location for Project Future focused on the Orlando vicinity, the ERA team investigated fifty properties, twenty-five of those having been researched in detail. A primary requirement was that the land consist of between three thousand and twelve thousand acres. The requirement excluded many parcels in western, northwestern, and northern parts of the city, areas dominated by citrus groves whose value exceeded $4,000 per acre—much too expensive for accumulating land of this size.

Fortunately, the study showed that large, single-owner land holdings and the placement of the new highways made southern Orlando the best location for the project. In particular, the report identified nine prospective parcels in this area for the development:

- A large parcel controlled by the Mormon Church
- A 6,000-acre parcel near East Tohopekaliga Lake
- A roughly 3,000-acre parcel owned by Major Realty Company, one of the largest landholders in Florida
- A 5,000-acre parcel known as the University Tract because of its proximity to an even larger parcel Florida State University was considering for a new campus in Orlando
- A 6,000-acre parcel known as the Highway Hub Tract, also near that proposed university location
- The 6,000-acre Lawson Ranch

- The Acorn River Ranch property located sixteen miles east of the city
- An 8,200-acre area known simply as Parcel 18
- A 12,000-acre parcel known as the Expressway Tract

The 1964 ERA report analyzed each property, focusing on proximity to highways, cost per acre, topography, size, and number of owners. Ultimately, the report ranked, in order of choice, the East Tohopekaliga property, the Expressway Tract, the Major Realty property, and the University Tract as the top four options. When ERA issued the report, its role was essentially complete. By late spring, Dick Morrow instructed Lund to write Nusbickel a letter thanking him for his help and advising that the client no longer needed FRL's services. As the year proceeded, the decision proved to be premature.

While none of the parcels identified in the 1964 ERA report would end up composing the complete boundaries of the Disney property, the Expressway Tract, together with several additional parcels, eventually comprised large portions of the actual project. Yet before compiling the land, the company found itself in the middle of a whirlwind of legal negotiations, cloaked in measures of extreme secrecy aimed at avoiding a rush of land speculation.

Chapter 3 1964

# The Early Florida Team and Potential Sites

While ERA conducted its work in late 1963, Disney was developing internal plans for the Florida project. Initially the company limited knowledge of the project to the select few who had participated in the November 27 meeting.

During that meeting, Robert Price Foster was charged with heading the legal efforts for Project Future. Well regarded in the company, he was the logical choice, having extensive experience with the amusement industry through his legal work at Disneyland. Soon enough, Foster's role grew to the point he ended up being the only Disney employee working full-time on the project. After receiving his assignment, Foster quickly set about to develop a game plan for investigating the viability of land acquisition in Florida. This involved obtaining as many public records as possible related to Florida property ownership. To help,

Foster limited his group to a select few, including his wife, also an attorney with a background in real estate law. Ultimately, Foster's group painstakingly evaluated more than fifty possibilities. The results served as the starting point for Disney's consideration of much of the land.

The team carefully reviewed detailed maps of available land that fit within the size and location parameters of the project. In doing so, they discovered numerous old subdivisions, some of which were no longer in use but still existed on the legal-record books. The problem was so prevalent that the Florida state legislature eventually passed a law providing for a simplified method to extinguish these subdivisions. Indeed, Disney itself would later use this power to disband subdivisions when it crafted the special governing legislation for Project Future.

### Paul Helliwell

Another key task was hiring local experts to assist the California-based Disney. To set this plan in motion, Disney turned to the Miami-based law firm of Helliwell, Melrose & De Wolf. The firm's prominent role in the project resulted from peculiar circumstances. Paul Helliwell, namesake of the Miami firm, received his law degree prior to joining the United States Army during World War II. Helliwell was assigned to the Office of Strategic Services [OSS], the U.S. intelligence agency formed during the war as a predecessor to the CIA. During Helliwell's tenure with OSS, he became friends with William Donovan, an attorney who headed the OSS. Donovan and Helliwell eventually led the OSS's intelligence operations in Europe. After the war, Donovan left the OSS and founded the law firm of Donovan, Leisure, Newton & Irvine based in New York. The firm represented Disney in a variety of national matters, including the Florida project. When the time came to hire Florida counsel for the project, Donovan recommended his former colleague Paul Helliwell to Disney.

In the spring of 1964, Helliwell received a call from Otto Charles "O.C." Doering, Jr., one of Donovan's partners and a personal friend of Helliwell. Like Helliwell, Doering had worked for Bill Donovan at the OSS as an executive officer and was a close confidant of Donovan. During the call, Doering asked Helliwell whether his firm was available to provide local counsel for a potentially significant land development in Florida. When Helliwell replied the firm was not currently representing any other major developers or landowners in the state, Doering somewhat cryptically told him to expect an important call soon.

Roughly ten days later, Doering called back and told Helliwell that a Mr. Foster would be contacting him. Doering would not share any information with Helliwell other than that Foster was from California. No reference whatsoever was made to Disney. Within a week of Doering's second call to Helliwell, Foster flew from New York, where he had been meeting with Walt Disney about the company's projects at the 1964-65 World's Fair, to Miami where he met with Helliwell for the first time. Initially, Foster did not disclose whom he worked for. However, following a short discussion in Helliwell's office, Foster shared that the project in question involved Disney and its efforts to develop a resort in the eastern United States. Foster went on to explain that the company would like Helliwell's help in researching properties in the range of seven thousand to ten thousand acres. In addition to his firm's legal assistance, Helliwell recommended Disney's hiring a local real estate expert to help with the search.

### Roy Hawkins

Subsequently, Foster conferred with Disney officials in California and received permission to retain a Florida real estate consultant and Helliwell sought recommendations from several acquaintances, all the while keeping Disney's identity in the strictest of confidence. Several business leaders including William Devere, then president of the First National Bank in the Palm Beach area, suggested Roy Hawkins, who had been active in the Florida real estate markets since the early 1920s and was serving as a director for a wide variety of companies, including American Bankers Life Company. Hawkins was familiar with executing large land deals throughout the state of Florida and was known as someone with discretion and savvy. Initially Hawkins was not told the client was Disney. Instead, Helliwell simply revealed the client was interested in obtaining thousands of acres of land in a general geographic area north of Palm Beach and south of Daytona Beach and the client did not want property located on the coast of the Atlantic Ocean or the Gulf of Mexico.

Not surprisingly, especially when considering the intelligence backgrounds of both Donovan and Helliwell, the Florida effort soon established policies to safeguard the project's secrecy. For instance, calls between Disney and the Miami firms were generally routed through the Donovan firm. This routing reduced the chance that an errant message or curious employee might make a direct connection between Disney and the land-acquisition efforts headed by the Helliwell firm. The company also took great care to avoid leaving a trail from California to Florida. Foster usually flew to Orlando through other cities rather than direct from California. His evasive measures were necessary because many persons, including Orlando area reporters, knew Foster was a key representative for the "mystery project" company.

At times the secrecy efforts led to comical situations, such as when Foster, operating under the name Bob Price, retreated into a another room to avoid reporters who showed up unannounced at the FRL office while Foster was there discussing land acquisition issues. The secrecy strategies ended up leading rumor chasers on a series of strange rabbit trails. On one occasion, Foster had traveled from Orlando to St. Louis to visit his mother in Kansas. This Orlando-to-St. Louis flight ramped up speculation that McDonnell Aircraft was behind the mystery project since the company's headquarters was located in St. Louis.

Of course, this state of wonder served Disney's goal of secrecy. And while the company did not explicitly engage in false practices, several of the key figures used subtlety to their full advantage. For example, during the heat of the rumors, Hawkins decided to take a vacation that included a trip to Seattle, Washington. Like many travelers, he sent postcards to friends back home. The arrival of the Seattle postcards to various Orlando acquaintances quickly fueled rumors that Boeing was the mystery industry—apparently based on little more than the fact that Hawkins was in Seattle and Seattle was then home to Boeing.

To avoid problems for Disney, a careful balance had to be struck when engaging in secret tactics. The company was well aware that the resourcefulness of the media and other rumor hunters could make playing overtly deceptive games a dangerous gambit. The local community seemed so intent on identifying who was behind the mystery effort that even one of Disney's own contacts at FRL later admitted he had called several companies, including Disney's California headquarters, asking to speak with a Bob Price.

While Foster's use of the Bob Price identity meant that nobody could track him to Disney, the rumor mill, now in full swing, did find a Bob Price at General Dynamics in San Diego. However, that rumor had a short lifespan. Once one of the rumor chasers spoke to that Bob Price on the phone, it became evident he was not the Bob Price traveling to Florida in search of property. Still, it was clear that Central Florida was not content to wait for the mystery company to reveal itself, meaning that Disney's efforts to acquire thousands of acres of land without disclosing its identity would continue to require large doses of discipline and secrecy.

# Narrowing Site Choices, Spring 1964

After Hawkins was retained in April 1964, he quickly began to identify properties throughout Florida that fit the client's large-acreage requirements. However, since he did not know the client was Disney and that it was seeking to build an amusement resort, numerous early properties he found were not good fits for the project. Thus, Helliwell suggested Hawkins could be more useful if he knew the client and the scope of the project. During a visit to Miami in June 1964, Foster and Tatum conferred with Helliwell about disclosing Disney's identity to Hawkins, and they agreed to do so.

## Sebring, Florida

Prior to then, Hawkins had located a parcel in Central Florida near Sebring. The site was promising enough that Foster himself flew into Miami and then drove to Sebring to tour the property. In addition, the Florida team gathered detailed information related to traffic counts and other empirical data. Unfortunately, the property was not located near any existing or planned highways, a key requirement for Disney, which anticipated many of the resort's visitors arriving by car.

Through the spring of 1964, Foster worked with his Florida colleagues and the California internal team reviewing available plats and other public documents to create a master map that identified approximately thirty potential sites in Florida for the Disney project. Foster, Hawkins, and the Florida team, which included Thomas DeWolf, another attorney with the Helliwell firm, had visited many of the sites at various times. Ultimately the group's efforts narrowed the project's location to four possibilities: Port St. Lucie, New Smyrna, Daytona, and the Orlando area. From the decision in November 1963 to move forward in Central Florida to this point roughly six months later, the company had accomplished a great deal. Plans were developing quickly.

### The Demetree Tract near Orlando

Near the end of April 1964, Foster traveled to Florida to inspect several properties in the central part of the state. The trip included a stop at a 12,440-acre parcel near Orlando known as the Demetree Tract, owned by brothers Jack and William Demetree and a third partner, Bill Jenkins. Hawkins was familiar with the property. During work for another client, he had learned about the site's availability. The Demetree parcel was particularly interesting. It not only included large acreage on a single site but was also located near the new I-4 and Florida Turnpike. Drive-in guests would have easy access to the Florida project.

That said, the site was not without its questions. In particular, according to Hawkins, the biggest challenge was that "all of Florida in 1964 was sort of in a depression and Orlando was one of the worst areas." Nevertheless, after returning to California in early May 1964, Foster and his Disney colleagues began to target the Demetree property, and they instructed Helliwell to begin drafting an option agreement for the parcel. Helliwell began preliminary work on the agreement before he left on a European vacation in mid-May.

## Daytona and New Smyrna, Florida

Although the Demetree property had become the company's primary focus, Disney's interest in Central Florida was serious enough that Foster again returned to Orlando in late May to tour other properties. To begin the trip, Foster, DeWolf, and Hawkins flew to Daytona Beach and rented a car. They inspected the Tomoka Ranch and parcels known as the Radford Cream property in New Smyrna and the Oak Hill Ranch. DeWolf also wanted to show the group some property his family owned near Crescent Lake, but the group never got there. Instead, they spent a large chunk of time at the Tomoka property in which Foster seemed especially interested.

## The Demetree Tract Revisited

After spending the night at the Sands Motel in Daytona, the group reconvened on the morning of May 22, 1964, and drove to Orlando where they met the Demetrees at the offices of Stockton, Whatley, & Davin, a mortgage and real estate company that Hawkins and the Demetrees had worked with in the past. Here the group loaded into Jeeps and toured the Demetree parcel. Foster was so impressed that he returned to California and reiterated the property's potential to Disney officials and Buzz Price.

The ultimate location for Project Future was getting closer.

Chapter 4 1964-1965

# Selecting Central Florida

---

With the Demetree property becoming a major target, Disney officials had to decide how to balance several interests. First, they wanted to continue keeping the company's involvement a secret. Also, because Disney himself had not yet officially decided to build a Florida project, the company wanted to limit the extent of its investment in case it decided not to move forward. Finally, the company wanted to begin locking down some type of legal interest in the prospective property because it knew that obtaining large chunks of land, even in undeveloped areas of Central Florida, could be time-consuming. They wanted to get ahead of the curve.

These issues led Disney to use option agreements at their legal tool of choice. An option agreement is basically a contract that allows a company to acquire legal rights short of actually purchasing a piece of land. Instead, a company simply pays for the right to be able to purchase the property at a set price within a certain timeframe. This allows for much more flexibility and is less expensive than an outright purchase. Purchasing options would save money and limit the amount of property Disney would need to divest if it should opt not to develop the project.

## Securing Options, Late Spring and Early Summer 1964

### The Demetree Tract

In late May 1964, Disney decided to begin negotiations in earnest with the Demetrees to acquire an option on their twelve-thousand-plus acres. During the second week of June, Foster gave Hawkins authority to purchase a thirty-day option on the Demetree parcel for up to $5,000. After Hawkins conveyed the offer to the Demetrees, they advised him that another Miami group was offering to purchase the property outright. The Disney group considered this competing offer serious enough that Foster and Tatum flew to Miami later that week to confer with the Florida-based team. The decision was made to offer more than simply a thirty-day option.

On June 18th, Helliwell traveled to Jacksonville with Foster to finalize negotiations with the Demetrees. Three days later, a longer option was completed in the name of Paul L.E. Helliwell, Trustee, for a price of $145 per acre. Disney had now secured a legal interest in the Demetree tract.

## The Bay Lake Tract

With the Demetree tract under option, Disney looked to obtain options on other contiguous properties. One of the most significant pieces was a parcel located near the existing Bay Lake. Ten individuals, who had used it primarily for recreation, owned the property. In addition to their personal use, they had also allowed civic groups to fish in the lake and to enjoy the property. At some point, the owners contemplated developing waterfront lots around the lake; but before their plans materialized, realtors from FRL approached them about selling the property.

As before, Disney's identity as the prospective purchaser remained undisclosed. The only information provided was that FRL's client wanted to obtain an option for the Bay Lake Tract. Negotiations led to an August 1964 option for the parcel. If the option were exercised, the purchase amount would be $250,000. Again, Paul L.E. Helliwell held the option as trustee. By securing the Bay Lake Tract option, Disney was closing in on the large acreage it sought for Project Future.

## The Hamrick Tract

The final large tract that Disney sought to secure was also located near Bay Lake. Owned by brothers Wilson and Carroll Hamrick, the roughly 2,700-acre parcel was referred to as the Hamrick Tract. The Hamrick brothers, whose business was growing citrus crops, had already talked to FRL realtors.

In July 1964, they listed the property for sale. Two months later, Disney secured an option for the parcel. In keeping with the company's goal of secrecy, this time the option was held in the name of David C. Nusbickel as trustee for the purchase price of $623,523.85. In January 1965 Nusbickel transferred the option to Paul Helliwell as trustee. With the Hamrick Tract in place, the vast majority of the total acreage for Project Future was now under option, all having occurred less than a year after Disney first decided to target Central Florida for the project.

## The Munger Subdivision

Even with the large parcels under option, Disney still encountered several legal hurdles, the most serious being the ability to obtain "clean" title to the land. The discovery of an early 1900s subdivision on part of the proposed Project Future property brought the issue to the forefront. While the land itself was almost abandoned—it included less than five houses, only one of which was occupied—a search of local records revealed large portions of the land had been subdivided over fifty years earlier. The area, in Orange County, was known as the Munger Subdivision after the former landowner who in 1912 and 1913 had subdivided much of the nineteen-thousand-plus acreage into five-acre plots. Disbanding the old subdivision would be difficult, but necessary since Walt himself decided the company needed to purchase much of the Munger land.

The problem was that Munger never took the appropriate steps to ensure the property was properly subdivided, evidenced by the fact that some of the "lots" were actually located in lakes or inaccessible swamp areas. Munger's apparent failure to survey the property meant the real dimensions of many lots varied from the dimensions stated in the recorded documents. This mess ensnared Disney because many of the lots in the Munger subdivision sat on part of the planned Project Future parcel. Robert Foster would later explain in his memoirs:

> *I could imagin[e] an army of distraught and enraged lot owners, their leader with Munger Subdivision Map in hand leading the charge, demanding the right to use alleged roadways crossing a golf course, through a hotel lobby and down Main Street, Disneyland East.*

Unless the land-title problems could be cleared up, the Florida project would be almost impossible to develop as planned. To solve the problem, a prospective buyer would have to purchase the subdivided parcels, petition the governing body to vacate the subdivision, and replat the land into an undivided parcel. After studying this approach, Disney concluded it was viable, although time-consuming and expensive. Eventually the company resolved most of the problems the Munger Subdivision created, but the process added an additional eight months to the company's overall land acquisition time frame.

## The Goldstein Property

Another problem involved a parcel owned by local resident Willie Goldstein and his wife.[1] The couple owned a thirty-seven-acre parcel that Disney wanted primarily because it was located on Bay Lake. Unfortunately, the Goldsteins were not interested in selling. Negotiations between Hawkins and the couple stalled, and Disney solicited the help of local business leaders, including Billy Dial and Martin Andersen, publisher of the Orlando Sentinel.

The tricky part was that in asking for help, Disney still remained an anonymous suitor, meaning the local leaders were asked to intercede on behalf of an unknown company. Nevertheless, Dial and Andersen sensed the company was legitimate and its project would benefit the community. Therefore, they reached out to other local leaders for help in convincing the Goldsteins to sell. While their initial efforts were not successful, eventually William Goldstein agreed to sell the couple's "little piece of heaven." Disney had completed a real coup: it had acquired the key parcel while keeping its identity confidential.

Beyond the challenge of securing the smaller parcels, Disney encountered a variety of other legal challenges, including questions related to oil and mineral rights.

## Securing Underground Ownership, Summer 1964

While Disney was able to obtain options for the Demetree land and other key parcels, those options were generally limited to the surface rights of the property. In many land transactions, these rights are sufficient, for the surface and underground rights are legally tied together. However, in some cases, these rights are separate. This separation usually occurs when a landowner sells a parcel's underground mineral rights apart from the surface rights.

### The Demetree Tract

For much of the Demetree property, this was the situation. Meaning that, though Disney had purchased an option from the Demetrees for the surface rights, the company had not secured the underground rights, which were not owned by the Demetrees. Instead, the mineral rights for the twelve-thousand-plus Demetree parcel were owned by Tufts College. Worse still, the college had previously refused the Demetrees' effort to purchase the mineral rights, a problem for the Demetrees because their option with Disney required that they either obtain the mineral rights or, if not possible, cooperate with Disney in obtaining them. Ultimately, if the college refused to sell the rights, Disney could walk away from the purchase in which case it would scuttle the entire project since the Demetree parcel composed such a large portion of the overall area.

The problem itself dated back to the 1940s when State Senator Irlo Bronson purchased the surface rights to the land from Tufts without also obtaining the underground rights. Often such a transaction makes little sense because whatever is developed on the surface of the land might be demolished if the holder of the mineral rights decides to exercise the underground rights. However, Bronson's family held large ranching interests and needed land for its cattle to graze. At the same time, oil and gas discoveries were increasing in the United States. The last thing Tufts wanted to do was sell out before it was sure valuable discoveries did not lurk under the ground. Bronson's need for the surface use and Tuft's desire to retain the underground interests made for an ideal fit.

Obviously Disney did not want the underground mineral rights because it planned to explore for natural resources on the property. Instead, the importance of the mineral rights centered on the fact that the holder of them also possessed the right to enter onto the property to explore for oil and minerals. If Disney were to develop the project, the holder of the mineral rights could disrupt the development by initiating exploration efforts.

In this case, Disney soon discovered the agreements were "the most onerous reservation of mineral rights" ever encountered. Therefore, realizing the high stakes, Disney developed a strategy for approaching Tufts about securing the underground rights. If successful, the company would then attempt to secure similar deals with other parties who held mineral rights to smaller pieces of the property.

The first step in Disney's strategy was to ascertain the likelihood of the existence of valuable mineral resources on the land. To make this determination, Disney reviewed public records in the State of Florida geologist's office. It found that companies had previously explored the land for both phosphorous and oil but in neither instance were the results promising enough to pursue. In fact, Disney secured a letter from Sun Oil, the company that had explored the land for oil and gas, confirming it had not found sufficient resources to exploit and would not be conducting any additional searches. This information would be important when approaching the mineral-right holders, for it indicated the rights were unlikely to yield much value.

Based on this information, Disney scheduled a meeting with board members from Tufts. Since purchasing the property from Florida State Senator Irlo Bronson in 1959, the Demetrees had worked hard to negotiate an agreement with Tufts on the mineral rights. They had made personal pleas, had hired attorneys to draft letters, and had met with key people who had connections with Tufts' trustees. Over the course of four years, though, none of the efforts were successful. Fortunately, Disney's luck seemed better. Paul Helliwell discovered a member of the finance committee for Tufts' board was a vice-president at First National Bank of Boston, an important fact considering that Helliwell and the bank's president were World War II colleagues.

In July 1964, Helliwell, Foster, and the Demetrees traveled to Boston to negotiate for the mineral rights. They and several Tufts trustees, including Helliwell's acquaintance at First National Bank of Boston, met in the conference room of the bank. Early on, the Tufts officials continued to seem disinterested in selling the mineral rights. The meeting did not seem to be going well, but a turning point occurred when Helliwell and the trustees excused themselves and left the conference room to confer privately. The Demetrees remained in the room, still concerned about the deal's prospects. After awhile, Helliwell and the Tufts officials returned and announced a deal had been struck. Had the agreement not been reached, plans to develop Disney's project in that location could have failed. In fact, according to Jack Demetree, the deal would not have been reached except for Paul Helliwell.

Ultimately, Disney purchased roughly six thousand acres worth of mineral rights while securing an option for another ten thousand acres. The purchase and option eliminated other persons' right to enter the property, something much more valuable to the project than the actual mineral rights. The end result is that a large chunk of today's Walt Disney World Resort was secured in a nondescript Boston conference room between Disney officials and key members of the Tufts College Board of Directors.

Upon obtaining these rights, Disney quickly secured stump-removal rights from Hercules Powder Company and smaller mineral rights from Wilson Cypress Company and the State of Florida. Now land-acquisition issues apparently would not derail the project.

With the key parcels under control, much of the remainder of the project's 1964 work was focused in California where Disney designers began crafting initial plans for the Florida resort. Helliwell met Roy Disney for the first time in the summer of 1964 when, after attending a business meeting in Atlanta, Roy Disney flew to Miami to get an update on the Florida efforts. Then in October 1964, Helliwell traveled to Burbank and met Walt Disney himself for the first time. Although they had secured options, Disney had not finally decided that the company would build a project in Florida. That key decision would not come until the next year.

The time frame from Fall 1964 until Spring 1965 was fairly quiet with the company doing most of its work on Project Future internally. That soon changed though. On May 20, 1965, Disney's identity as the potential purchaser was addressed in an Orlando Sentinel story. The paper, while reporting on the Hamrick transaction, stated:

There has been one consistent rumor that the land is being purchased for a second East Coast Disneyland attraction, but little credence is given this in view of the fact that Walt Disney himself, in a recent statement to The Orlando Sentinel while on a visit to Cape Kennedy, said he was spending $50 million to expand his California attraction and had neither the time nor the talent to look for a second venture. In short, Mr. Disney said he already had his hands full.

On June 12, 1965, the paper's gossip columnist Charlie Wadsworth further challenged Disney's secrecy with either an extremely good guess—or an extremely well-sourced rumor:

*Here's rumor no.63 (or is it 64A?) about the mystery industry: Nearly all of the companies named in the earlier speculation will participate in a plan to put together a huge, life-sized model of the city of the future, depicting what life will be like about the year*

*2050, say. Walt Disney would furnish the*
*ideas and put the overall package together.*

Although the details were not quite right, the columnist's suggestion sounded very much like Walt's plan for his City of Tomorrow as the signature feature of the Florida project. His elaborate vision for Central Florida seemed to be slowly coming out of secrecy before the company had even exercised its land options for the project. If Disney's identity were leaked and worked its way into the papers before the company could finalize purchases, the whole project could crumble, for speculators would likely bid up the land to outrageous prices.

The company was so concerned about its identity being revealed that it dispatched Helliwell to meet with Billy Dial, the local Orlando banker and business leader who had helped with acquiring the Goldstein property. In Dial's office, Helliwell claimed, "Bill, we have got a problem. This big industry wants to come into Florida, I can't tell you who it is. It is top secret . . . it is something that any town in Florida would give its right arm to get." Helliwell went on to explain that, while the mystery company had large key parcels under contract, it still needed to purchase an interest in smaller parcels.[1]

Helliwell told Dial quite succinctly, "If this leak is publicized, [the project] is dead."

Dial trusted Helliwell and believed the prospective project would be a boon for the Orlando area. He suggested to Helliwell a visit with Martin Anderson, publisher of the Orlando Sentinel. Hearing about the dilemma, Anderson made a critical decision. He gathered his reporters and editors and instructed them not to publish the mystery company's identity if they discovered it. While the decision surely caused an uproar in the newsroom, it gave Disney necessary time to anonymously complete several remaining purchases.

The options Disney had secured gave it legal rights to purchase the parcels but did not actually give it ownership. To obtain that, Disney had to convert the options to purchases. This meant spending large amounts of money to complete the transactions.

## The Bronson Parcel in Osceola County

Disney's strategy of obtaining options rather than purchasing parcels outright was used for the project's largest parcels except one, a large swath of property in Osceola County owned by State Senator Irlo Bronson, the same individual who had sold the Demetrees their parcel. Disney assigned responsibility for obtaining the Bronson land to Hawkins. To help, Hawkins reached out to an old friend, R.B. "Bunn" Gautier and asked him to contact his senate colleague Bronson about the property.

With Hawkins standing nearby, Gautier called Bronson and told him that someone wanted to discuss his property in Osceola County. Gautier then handed the phone to Hawkins, who asked if he and Gautier could drive to Bronson's Kissimmee home and talk with him about the property. Bronson said he was heading out of town but would be glad to meet them at his motel in Port St. Lucie the next morning. The next day Hawkins and Gautier drove to Bronson's hotel and tried to close the deal. Bronson, a cattle rancher who did not believe the land was well suited for ranching, wanted $100 per acre for the ten thousand acres. The price seemed reasonable, and Hawkins arranged a tour of the property. After touring the land, Disney officials quickly moved to secure it.

On May 3, 1965, the company purchased 8,380 acres from Senator Bronson for $900,000. Technically, the sale was between Bronson's, Inc., and the Latin-American Development and Management Corporation, a dummy company for which Paul Helliwell served as the lead contact. Although the transaction again sparked rumors about a mystery industry coming to town, Disney's use of the dummy corporation allowed it to remain anonymous even after purchasing the land. In fact, at the time many persons in Orlando had changed their mind about the mystery client being Disney and were predicting the transactions were the work of the reclusive Howard Hughes.

### The Bay Lake, Demetree, and Hamrick Tracts

Later that month the company also completed its transaction for the Bay Lake tract, again using a dummy corporation, Bay Lake Properties, Inc., which purchased the 1,250-acre parcel for $250,000 from Bay Isles Associates, the group of ten investors. Next up was exercising the option on the Demetree property, which was conveyed to Reedy Creek Ranch, Inc., on June 22 for $1,806,364.33. Two days later Disney exercised the Hamrick option with the property being conveyed to Tomahawk Properties, Inc., another dummy corporation controlled by Disney, for $561,171.46.

By June 1965, Disney had acquired actual title or options for twenty-seven thousand acres of land, comprising roughly forty-three square miles. Amazingly, Disney had been able to obtain all of this land for slightly more than $5 million—under $200 an acre. Disney had used the dummy corporations—Reedy Creek Ranch, Inc., Bay Lake Properties, Inc., Tomahawk Properties, Inc., Ayefour Corporation, and the Latin American Development and Management Corporation—as yet another part of its strategy to maintain secrecy during the purchase process. The five Florida corporations held title to the property, and a Disney-controlled Delaware corporation known as Compass East owned each of the five corporations' stock.

The vision for this "raw" land on which one inhabitable house remained included theme parks, an industrial park, an airport, conventional housing, and Disney's City of Tomorrow. But before site work could begin, the company still had to overcome challenging legal and regulatory hurdles. By the summer of 1965, the most important task facing Disney had shifted from acquiring the land to figuring out how to legally accomplish the company's goals for the land. The small nucleus of the Disney team would have to be expanded.

Foster noted in his memoir:

> *Project "X" had been a project with a one man in house staff, supported by my stalwart companion Floridians Helliwell and Hawkins. Obviously, the formidable task before us was more than we three were able to handle. The inner circle of Project "X" had to be expanded.*

This expansion included outside attorneys Helmut Firth and John Baity, industrial engineer Tad Crowell, tax expert George Sullivan, and General William Potter, who was completing his role as an executive of the New York World's Fair. Together this core group, among others, would transform Project Future from an idea to a reality.

Chapter 5 Summer 1965

# Final Decisions

---

Following two years of land acquisition, the Summer of 1965 found Project Future entering a new phase, the decision-making period during which the company would select, among other things, a legal and regulatory strategy for developing the massive new project. The week of June 14, 1965, marked a key event in the process. The expanded group of Disney officials, including the company's outside board members whom Roy Disney had invited, convened for a four-day seminar to discuss implementation strategies related to Project Future. Foster acted as the event's lead organizer and moderator. Walt himself attended only the opening and closing sessions but was provided with daily transcripts of the meeting.

## Implementation Strategies

Gathering in Disney's third floor conference room for what Foster referred to as "our own constitutional convention," he opened the seminar by describing the unprecedented scope of the project. Indeed, the 27,400-acre property measuring eleven miles long by seven miles wide constituted "an undertaking of the greatest magnitude this company has ever considered." Officials at the meeting estimated the overall investment for infrastructure and facilities would exceed $100 million. The company anticipated that $30 million of the total cost would come from corporations purchasing the right to exhibit their products at the project.

The week's format was straightforward: Take the proposed project and work it through the business and regulatory development process hypothetically. To accomplish the method, the group centered its analysis on two simple questions: What are the impediments to developing this project in Florida and how do we overcome them? Significantly, the questions applied not only to the initial Magic Kingdom theme park but also to every other facet of the entire project, right down to the technical logistics and infrastructure. The exercise was extremely broad considering that the then scope of the project included residential, office, and industrial components in addition to the commercial entertainment portion.

One major item on the meeting's agenda related to the importance of counties in Florida and their control over taxes. During the seminar, Disney officials considered how

Orange and Osceola counties would assess and tax the property during its development stages. In particular, the group was keen on making sure the counties would not assess taxes based on the prospective value of the property as a resort. Helliwell explained that Florida law treated land as unimproved for tax purposes until it reached 75 percent completion as of January 1st of a given year and that county tax authorities would not tax an improvement until it was actually used. The possibility was important for a phased project such as this one in which a single phase might be completed but not operational for as long as a year. To increase the likelihood of these results, Helliwell floated the idea of seeking an Attorney General opinion, for those opinions carried significant weight in Florida at the time.

Other legal and regulatory issues discussed during the seminar included:

- Protection of the Disney trademark within Florida
- The possibility of an involuntary annexation of the project by the City of Orlando or another city in the area
- The liability and tax benefits of establishing Disney's own drainage district
- The applicability of local planning and zoning ordinances to the site
- The applicability of existing building codes
- The issue of whether the waterways within the property would be classified as navigable for control purposes

Regulatory concerns about the project were not limited to external issues. The company also had to address a variety of internal issues such as "the relationship between existing Disney subsidiaries and the project." This would involve deciding which specific entity, or more likely entities, would own, operate, design, engineer, and build the project. These questions themselves raised legal issues, for the entities, many of whom would be engaging in professional services, would likely require various Florida licenses.

In addition, during the seminar Disney expressed concern that the small number of residents in Orlando would make operating the Florida resort much different from Disneyland with its large Los Angeles population. Even more significant was Disney's emphasis on controlling the area so that it would not become a jungle of signs, lights, and fly-by-night operations that would distract the project's audience. Once again, the theme of control was introduced and would serve as one of the leading factors in decision-making related to the project.

During this meeting, Helliwell made the early suggestion that Disney create its own municipality for the project "so that we can control our own destiny." However, Disney officials expressed some concern that creating a city could force the company to cede authority to the newly-created municipality. In response, Helliwell explained Disney could form the municipality using a special act approved by the state legislature, a strategy that would give the company much more control over the municipality's operating charter. Creating its own municipality would help streamline the tedious review-and-approval process for "everything from permits for a parade to a license to sell popcorn or balloons on the street."

Another important problem that could be solved by creating a municipality was the matter of utilities. The company had discussed creative partnerships with RCA, General Electric, AT&T, and the Bell System about designing state of the art power and communication systems. However, the counties, as well as the Florida Telephone Company and Florida Power Company, controlled utility franchises in the area. Serious questions existed regarding whether these utility providers could meet the financial and technical requirements for a project of this scale. As a result, Disney concluded that it should attempt to provide its own utility service.

However, even this idea met with a regulatory challenge. While a private company could generally provide its own utilities without oversight of the Florida Public Utilities Commission, the company would be subject to the Commission's jurisdiction if utilities were extended to third parties. This concern was a potential problem, for the existing utility regulations in Florida were very conventional in nature and, therefore, would not be conducive to the type of innovation Disney aspired to. And, since third party lessees would occupy various parts of the project, if Disney wanted to innovate beyond what the Commission would allow, the only option would be to create a municipality because cities were generally exempt from the Commission's oversight. Considering all of these factors, the municipality idea appeared to gain the group's support. In particular, the increased amount of control resonated with the Disney officials so much so that participants at the meeting noted "[i]f a municipality is not formed the controls which would otherwise be granted to it would be vested in the county (over which we would have no control)."

While the idea of creating a municipality piqued the group's interest, at least one Disney official suggested that cities, if established, should exclude residential properties, for they could dilute the company's influence. Once again, Helliwell offered a possible legal solution: limit voting rights in the municipalities to landowners. This solution would allow for leased residential units without the company diluting its control via voting rights. To support the strategy, Helliwell pointed to three Florida cases that provided precedent for the approach.

Another alternative that Helliwell proposed was to establish separate municipalities for the proposed residential areas and the proposed commercial/amusement components of the project. This alternative would allow the company to include potentially lucrative residential sales in the project without giving the prospective residents any control of the separate commercial operations.

Little did Helliwell know, Walt was biased against the idea before it was ever introduced. His bias resulted from the experiences of Jules Stein, a friend who at the time was a lead executive of Universal Studios. Stein had cautioned Walt against creating new cities as part of his Florida project. This caution resulted from trouble Stein had encountered after incorporating Universal City, a parcel of land the Studios owned in the county outside the Los Angeles city limits. In that case, both the county and the city repeatedly pestered Stein because of his decision to separately incorporate as a municipality. Stein advised Walt the hassle of having his own city would end up being a major burden.

Nevertheless, participants in the meeting carefully considered how the municipal structure in Florida could help meet their goal of maintaining control over the project. The group realized creating a municipality was critical, and eventually Walt relented. Since the process of establishing a municipal corporation in Florida required upward of six months, the meeting attendees set December as the date for completing a draft charter for the cities. The charter would address the structure for managing them and the scope of power granted to them—with land use, taxation, and bonding authority being among the company's chief interests in establishing its own city.

Despite the large number of challenges the group identified, the Project Future seminar took on a positive tone in many respects. For instance, Helliwell suggested the project would not need much in the way of state legislation—a claim that would eventually prove quite premature—and any state legislation it might need would be helped by a positive political climate for the project—a prediction that would prove extraordinarily accurate. Meanwhile, Hawkins explained that Florida's State Development Commission was eager to cooperate in making the proposal a reality. He was sure the Commission would lend support, for it had recently backed large Pratt-Whitney, General Electric, and Aerojet projects in the state. Indeed, Hawkins went so far as to proclaim that from a business development perspective, the "potential is unlimited" for Project Future.

The three-day meeting concluded with attendees considering a broad spectrum of other issues, including the creation of an atomic energy facility, banks, an insurance company, and even an airport for the project. Ultimately, the June 1965 Project Future seminar set the agenda for Disney's next legal and regulatory steps as it continued to refine strategies for retaining control over as many aspects of the massive project as possible. Indeed, by the end of the meeting, the official announcement that Disney was coming to Central Florida was just months away.

However, the Project Future meeting did not tie up all potential loose ends. In particular, although the consensus was to build in Florida, it was not unanimous. One of the meeting's key participants, Card Walker, opposed locating the project in the Sunshine State. He continued to press for building the project in the Washington D.C. area and also continued to express interest in the St. Louis project even though those negotiations were faltering. Fortunately, his argument to build elsewhere failed to carry the day. If Project Future was to be built, the meeting's participants decided Florida would be the location.

On June 25, 1965, the Orlando Evening Star ran a headline that simply read "'Let's Go!' 2nd Stage Launched."

In the article, Helliwell confirmed the still-anonymous Disney had completed nearly all of the land purchases for the mystery project. Although actual details as to what the project would involve remained secret, "Phase Two," according to Helliwell, would now commence with an emphasis on planning and engineering. Yet before that phase could happen, Disney faced another major challenge: maneuvering through the political and legal landscapes of Florida.

# Clearing the Political and Legal Hoops, 1965-1968

### A "Super District"

In 1965, Florida counties maintained a great deal of power primarily because of their taxing authority. Disney officials briefly discussed the idea of creating the company's own county. However, after researching the legal requirements, they decided such an effort would be nearly impossible. Paul Helliwell's recommendation that Disney establish its own municipality continued as the primary regulatory strategy until Attorneys Foster and DeWolf collaborated on the idea of utilizing Florida's existing special district law to create an improvement district.

The improvement district would represent a win-win for both the company and the counties. Disney could retain more control over the project than a municipality would provide, and Orange and Osceola Counties would avoid the cost of installing the massive infrastructure the project would require. Ultimately, the improvement district would absorb the financial burden of the project while the county governments would realize the financial benefit of increased values in land surrounding the Disney site.

Special Districts in Florida have a long and varied history. The first such districts trace their origins back to the Road, Highway, and Ferry Act of 1822 passed by the early Florida Territorial Legislature to facilitate the construction of transportation routes through the wet, swampy lands of this southern outpost. Following Florida's statehood in 1845, the legislature passed an act which created Florida's first legislative special district, one that empowered the financing of wetland reclamation through special assessments upon landowners.

Expanding on this concept, Disney developed a strategy that increased the traditional scope of drainage districts into an entity empowered to govern a broader array of issues beyond drainage. Indeed, DeWolf's research on drainage districts would ultimately serve as the regulatory basis for the "super district." However, before proceeding with the plans, Walt himself had to be convinced this course was the best strategy. This responsibility fell to Foster.

Knowing Walt would have little patience for a presentation filled with legal and regulatory technicalities, Foster prepared a series of flash cards outlining over twenty regulatory subjects that required attention. He then scheduled a meeting in which he would present the idea to Walt and Dick Morrow, the company's head attorney. To start with, Foster placed a large card on a wall that read "Super District." Under this heading, he placed each of the flash cards that described a regulatory role that could legally be assigned to the improvement district. The remaining cards represented areas of governance requiring a more conventional local government structure; that is, either under the purview of a new municipality or that of the existing counties.

Concluding his presentation, Foster recounted in his memoirs the moment when Disney embraced the "super district" strategy:

> As I approached the end of the presentation, having all the district's authority explained and the cards representing municipality powers remaining, Walt fulfilled his reputation by commenting 'My God Bob you speak slowly, all of these left over [will] have to be put in a city.'. . . It was then and there that the governmental structure for Walt Disney World, the Reedy Creek Improvement District superimposed with two municipalities[,] had its conception.

Now that Walt had approved the strategy, the next step would be to get the state legislature's approval, a process that would outlive the genius himself.

While the improvement-district approach provided a novel framework for organizing the project, Walt's desire to control the environment competed with the desire to develop the massive land holdings. An example was residential housing.

## Land Ownership and Voting Power

Walt's original vision for the project included private housing for employees of Project Future. By 1971, this vision began to take shape when the Buena Vista Land Company, a subsidiary of Walt Disney Productions, started construction on a 3,800-acre portion of the property that would include private residences such as houses, apartments, and town homes. In a 1971 interview, Roy Disney explained the rationale for the effort. "This gets us into developing, building up the lots, and from there we gradually move into the whole EPCOT idea."

Still though, Disney officials realized private housing within the Florida project could dilute their control over the development. If Disney wanted to maintain quality control, the company would have to find a way to limit the voting power of the private residents.

This issue placed Disney in a precarious situation. All along, the ability to control voting within the district was a key requirement for the company. To do so, Disney intended to limit the ability of prospective Reedy Creek residents from participating in the governance of the district through voting powers. One method for accomplishing this goal was to allocate voting power by land ownership. With Disney as the predominant landowner, the company could control votes related to the district. Yet the U.S. Supreme Court's recent rulings related to voting rights continued to vex this idea. As a result, Disney eventually abandoned plans for individually-owned residential units in the project. The units that Roy Disney announced in 1971 later became vacation lodging.

However, even with these uncertain issues swirling around this unprecedented project, the company's Florida efforts were about to enter a new phase. A local reporter was prepared to break the big news that the mystery industry entering Central Florida was none other than the Walt Disney Company.

Chapter 6 Fall 1965

# The Mystery Client

---

Throughout the summer and into the fall of 1965, the Florida news media focused on the identity of the mystery corporation buying large chunks of Central Florida land. Disney though was not ready to reveal its involvement. That summer during a press conference after Walt had toured NASA's facilities in Cape Canaveral, Florida, the media asked Disney whether his company was coming to Florida. Walt vaguely denied any involvement. Yet, this loose denial only temporarily delayed the inevitable. Both reporters and business leaders in Florida were narrowing in on Disney as the potential mystery company.

# Revealing the Florida Project, Fall 1965

## The Media's Guess, October 1 and 17

On October 1, 1965, Helliwell, while on a trip to Central Florida, announced that his client would reveal itself and its plans during a November 15 press conference in Orlando. But the local media would not allow the company to play by its own timetable.

For starters, gossip columnist Wadsworth reported on October 13 and 19 that anecdotal evidence indicated Disney was the mystery company. His suggestion was based on the off-hand comment by a participant at a recent business meeting in Anaheim, California. The participant claimed Disney had recently purchased large amounts of land in Florida. Wadsworth also noted larger-than-normal amounts of Disney stock were being traded, something that might reasonably occur in advance of a major company announcement.

Then on Sunday, October 17, Orlando Sentinel reporter Emily Bavar wrote an article that seemed to end the mystery. Bavar, editor of Florida Magazine, the paper's special Sunday publication, had been assigned to cover Disneyland's tenth anniversary. While on the assignment, Bavar interviewed Walt Disney in his Burbank office. During the meeting, Disney would neither confirm nor deny whether the company had purchased land in Central Florida.  Later, Bavar reported that he "adroitly hedged direct questions concerning it." Still though, the reporter noticed Disney seemed to know a great deal more about

Central Florida than someone having no interest in the area. Disney's quick recall about weather, traffic, and tourism in Central Florida convinced her that Disney was the mystery company.

Ironically, while Bavar was putting the pieces together, the Sentinel's publisher had previously, and secretly, been briefed on the matter and asked to stall the revelation in the paper. This delay gave Disney time to compile the needed land before rampant speculation broke out. However, even editors could not delay Bavar's well-reasoned story.

When the original Bavar story broke, Foster and General Potter happened to be in Orlando on business that included a helicopter tour of the property. Potter, who had met and worked with Disney at the 1964-65 New York World's Fair, had recently been hired by the company to direct development of the Florida project. Upon waking that Sunday morning, Potter went to the lobby of the Robert Meyer Hotel where he was staying and there discovered the Orlando Sentinel story identifying Disney as the secret company. Realizing the significance of the story, Potter called back to California and informed Card Walker the secret was out.

### The Governor's Announcement, October 25

Governor Burns's office was soon calling Disney and demanding that, if the company was indeed coming to Florida, the governor and his administration needed to know. Realizing the secret campaign was over, Walt himself decided to go public. Rather than wait until the November

15 press conference, the company quickly set in motion plans to officially announce involvement later that week in Miami. Governor Burns was scheduled to address the Florida League of Municipalities Convention on Monday, October 25, and Disney officials decided the convention would be a good time to reveal their Florida project. Foster and Potter immediately flew to Miami and briefed the governor and his advisors. In a clever political move, Disney gave the honor of revealing the company's plans to Governor Burns. With Hawkins, Helliwell, Potter, Foster, and Dick Morrow in the audience, the governor announced to a roar of applause that Walt Disney Productions was coming to Florida and bringing with it a massive new development for the Sunshine State.

With the news out, the project took a major turn. Gone was the need for secret corporations, code names, and plane trips. Another advantage of being public was the company could now engage Florida officials more directly about government assistance in bringing the project to fruition.

Disney soon initiated a concerted effort to inform state leaders of the benefits the Disney project would bring to Florida. One such instance involved the state Comptroller Fred "Bud" Dickinson and ten other Florida officials traveling to Disney's California headquarters in December 1965 for a three-day fact-finding trip related to Disneyland's operations. The goal was to demonstrate that Florida's existing regulations, such as building codes, did not sync well with Disney's unique attractions and overall project design. The strategy seemed to work for, upon returning to

Florida, Dickinson reported he was "very impressed with the spirit of cooperation between our state government and the Walt Disney executives and technicians." Disney's investment in bringing Florida officials to California was yielding early returns.

Another key part of Disney's regulatory strategy for the Florida project was to adopt a customized building and design code that would ultimately be stricter in substance than existing codes but more creative in matters such as permissible materials. A customized regulatory code would enable Disney to produce innovative designs that were still deeply rooted in providing for guest safety.

The October 25 announcement generated a great deal of excitement. However, because the event was hastily arranged, exact details were sparse. They would have to wait until Disney's November 15 press conference in Orlando.

### November 14, 1965

Walt and Roy Disney, along with company executives, arrived in Tallahassee in advance of the official press conference in Orlando the next day. That evening the group joined a cadre of business and political leaders from Florida for a reception at the governor's mansion. Disney gave a short talk and posed for pictures with attendees. The mood was festive in anticipation of the next day's big event.

The previous week Governor Burns had flown from Tampa to California to meet with Disney executives about the big announcement. When he arrived back in Tampa on

November 10, reporters met him at the airport, wanting information about the Disney project. Burns was tight-lipped and stingy with details, though. He simply assured them that additional information would become public during the upcoming press conference in Orlando. Burns's coyness increased the already high anticipation surrounding the event.

## November 15, 1965

On the morning of November 15, the Disney group and Governor Burns flew to Orlando by private plane. Upon landing, they proceeded to the Cherry Plaza Hotel where the press conference was to be held. Tickets for this invitation-only gathering were highly-sought after with key players throughout Florida jockeying for the opportunity to attend. The group first gathered in the governor's suite for a small, private luncheon. From there, they proceeded to the hotel's Egyptian Room for a meeting with select state business and political leaders. Here Disney discussed his ideas in broad terms and presented a short slide show that further introduced the company to Florida's decision-makers.

## The Press Conference

After a short break, Disney and Governor Burns returned to the Egyptian Room for a 5:00 p.m. press conference. As the crowd packed into the room, expectations were high, probably overly so considering that the actual planning and design for the project was still in its nascent stages. During the event, Walt offered few details other than predicting a price tag of $100 million for the project and acknowledging that his vision included both a real working city and planned entertainment components. He also acknowledged the daunting challenge the company faced in taking on such a large and diverse project.

"This is a tremendous challenge to us," he said. "We are terrified by the project. Just think! We need one hundred million dollars just to get the show on the road."

Clearly, Walt understood implementing his vision for Project Future would be one of the company's most difficult challenges to date.

### Post-Conference

After the press conference, in a receiving line at a private reception in the hotel's Fountain Terrace Room, Disney, the governor, and others greeted well-wishers. When the reception broke up, Walt and his delegation departed for what had apparently become their favorite hotel, the Robert Meyer. As he had done the morning of the press conference, the next day he headed out to see the Florida property. Dressed casually and accompanied by key Disney officials, he toured the site by boat and jeep, genuinely excited to have so much land at his disposal. After touring the site, Walt headed back to California while other advisors, including Roy Disney, stayed behind to work on details. The possibilities were expansive. By early 1966, Disney would take several more quiet trips back to Florida to tour the property and to continue the planning efforts.

For his part, Governor Burns was so excited about Disney's locating in Florida that he admitted to purchasing blocks of Disney stock, an investment that would later pay off handsomely for him.

Meanwhile, that evening Billy Dial, the local leader who had shepherded the project through some key moments, hosted the remaining Disney officials for dinner. During dinner, Roy Disney thanked Dial for his assistance during the critical junctures.

"Bill, you have been awfully helpful to us down here; you have been awfully nice and all that," Roy Disney said, "but when are you going to ask me for our banking business?"

"That is secondary," Dial answered. "The main deal was to get you here."

With so many people already trying to get in with Disney, Dial's approach was refreshing and Roy Disney offered Disney's Florida banking business on the spot. Dial gladly accepted.[2]

**Chapter 7** 1965-1968

# Drain a Swamp and Build a World

---

With the project no longer a secret, Disney started early site development. In fact, the company was so ready to get started that it did not even wait for the formal November 15 press conference before beginning.

By the last week of October 1965, Roy Hawkins's close acquaintance Olin Edwards and his Florida-based Edwards Construction Company had already cleared several hundred acres of property. Disney had also hired the West Palm Beach engineering firm of Gee and Jenson to begin site and drainage studies for the project, much of which was marsh and wetland at the time. Senator Irlo Bronson even remained involved, this time as a landscaping consultant for the project.

Another change was that almost immediately after the announcement, delegations of Florida leaders began traveling to Anaheim to see first-hand the Disney theme park. The delegates' trips to Disneyland were the start of a period in which Disney furnished a large number of complimentary tours and admissions to a wide range of Floridian political and business officials. They included officials from the Central Florida counties that would be most affected by the project, including State Senator Beth Johnson whose district included parts of the Disney property. Disney's goal was to bring the groups to California early on to demonstrate that Disneyland was of the highest quality, the type of well-planned project Floridians would certainly embrace.

During the post-announcement time, Disney officials continued to visit Florida for follow-up meetings. One key meeting involved a February 1966 trip by Tatum, Foster, Morrow, and Potter. Helliwell and Hawkins joined them, and the team discussed technical issues such as infrastructure and roads, two issues that would play a significant role in determining whether the project would move forward. At the end of that trip, they met with Governor Burns for two hours and, now that the initial excitement had somewhat died down, began to detail their strategies for developing the Florida project.

## Creating the Plans, Summer 1966

While Walt had many ideas about what to include in Project Future, most of them were preliminary. It was now time to begin turning those ideas into concrete plans. For this task, in June 1966 Disney turned to Marvin Davis to craft an initial master plan for the project. Davis's task was to incorporate Disney's various ideas into a cohesive whole, to develop an overall site plan for the theme park, a manmade lagoon near Bay Lake, and several areas that would house recreation and lodging facilities.

Davis's assignment also included the land set aside for the EPCOT complex. This involved developing a site plan that would incorporate a town center area for an estimated thirty thousand residents as well as support structures such as warehouses and parking facilities for visitors. All in all, Davis was now the chief planner for implementing Disney's vision.

The epicenter for the planning effort was the Florida Room, a tall room in Burbank with walls covered to the ceiling by the various plans for the project site. This secretive space, to which few were granted admission, would become the birthplace of the EPCOT film, a Disney-created production that outlined the conceptual plans for the project. The EPCOT film would turn out to be Disney's final film, one that played an important role in convincing Florida officials that the state should approve a creative, new legislative package for this unique effort.

Over the course of the next six years leading up to the October 1971 grand opening, Disney would reclaim thousands of acres of wetlands while installing state of the art drainage and water control infrastructures. However, before the company moved too deep into this development phase, it needed key legal and legislative commitments from local and state authorities.

Chapter 8 1966-1971

# The Legal and Legislative Years

Soon after rumors of Disney's involvement in Central Florida were confirmed, property values in the area began to skyrocket. Everyone wanted to be near Disney's project and the large number of guests it was likely to bring to the region. But before anything could be built, Disney had to shepherd its regulatory package through the state legislature.

## Preparing a Legislative Package

### Highways and Roads

Almost immediately, the project ran into its first political challenge. On November 2, 1965, Floridians voted down a proposed $300 million bond issue for roads. A large portion of the bond issue would have been assigned to highway and access improvements in Central Florida, something that was critical for Disney since its forecasts projected a large drive-

in visitor base. Reports were indicating that over 80 percent
of guests would arrive by automobile, and the company
needed to make sure that adequate road infrastructure
was in place for the fairly rural project site. Immediately
after the vote defeating the bond measure, Governor Burns
met with Disney officials who were in Florida at the time.
The goal was to develop an alternate strategy for the new
highway infrastructure that was critical to the project. So
important was the matter that Governor Burns later traveled
to California and met personally with Walt about how to
move forward after this unexpected development.

## Taxation

Another early governance issue confronting the project
was its tax status. Most of the land Disney purchased was
currently being taxed at a lower agricultural rate since it was
undeveloped. The company needed the property to remain
taxed at the agricultural level until it opened instead of
when construction began. Taxation at the lower rate would
result in a significant savings during the five years the
project would be under development. To press this point, in
early November 1965 Hawkins and Helliwell met with local
tax and government officials in both Orange and Osceola
County. After visiting with the counties' tax assessors and
members of the Osceola County Commission, the parties
seemed to reach, even if only informally, an agreement—
another early problem resolved. Now it was almost time to
begin preparing the legislative package the company would
submit to state legislators to begin the project in earnest.

## The Reedy Creek Drainage District, Spring 1966

Before submitting the legislative package, Disney needed to complete a small but important preliminary step, one that would play a disproportionately large role in bringing the project to fruition. This step involved establishing a drainage district that would manage water control for the property. By this time, General Potter had been placed in charge of the land management and development portion of the project. Based on his earlier experience leading the Panama Canal effort, Potter knew that unless the company efficiently controlled the infrastructure and engineering process, the project could become entangled in regulatory gridlock.

To avoid a gridlock, Potter pushed hard for spending money on early drainage and engineering studies to understand what exactly the company faced in reclaiming the land for development. The Gee & Jensen engineering firm offered its findings in a report dated December 1965. The firm also made the political recommendation that Disney should establish its own Chapter 298 Drainage District, named after the section of the Florida Code in which the district regulation was found. Under this structure, Disney could control most of the decision-making related to drainage in the area since Chapter 298 apportioned that authority based on land ownership. Because Disney owned nearly all of the land, it would be able to control the process by out-voting any of the few remaining landowners who might oppose the process.

This idea of control once again instinctively appealed to Disney officials, and in March 1966 the company petitioned the Circuit Court of the Ninth Judicial District to create the Reedy Creek Drainage District pursuant to Chapter 298 of the Florida Statutes. In mid-April, before the Court had ruled on the petition, Potter called a key meeting with Osceola and Orange County commissioners at the Robert Meyer motel, the same location at which Potter had first learned about Bavar's story in October 1965. Here Potter explained to the commissioners and flood-control officials that the approval of a Disney-controlled drainage district was critical for the project to move forward. He also noted that the cost of the entire project was now estimated at nearly $500 million up from the $100 million number used at the November 15, 1965, press conference.

After a court hearing attended by Bob Foster and Roy Disney, the Court approved Disney's application for a new drainage district. Approval allowed Disney to begin the time-consuming effort of draining and reclaiming much of the land so that actual site construction would be possible. However, this initial legal victory was tempered by growing legislative problems, none of which were caused by Disney but each of which could conceivably derail the project.

## Surviving Unexpected Political Changes, Fall 1966

In June 1964, as part of an ongoing lawsuit, the United States Supreme Court ordered the Florida legislature to reapportion its state House and Senate districts. The state legislature responded in 1965 by adopting a new reapportionment plan. However, this solution was short-lived, for the United States Supreme Court overturned the plan in 1966. In response, Governor Burns called a special session in March 1966 to set new legislative districts in advance of the scheduled April 1966 primary election. He pushed for Disney to include its legislative package in the special session, but the company declined, for its final plans were incomplete.

Even had the plan been ready, Disney faced a bigger problem. Because of the reapportionment, the company did not know who would end up being in the legislature when it submitted its package, much less who would represent Orange and Osceola Counties. The latter issue was a major problem because, under Florida practice, the local legislative delegation would be the first to hear and consider Disney's legislative requests. If the local delegation voted in opposition, the full legislature would also likely vote against the requests. As a result, the company was forced to consult with the current legislators. Disney officials could only hope that these legislators would survive reapportionment, knowing full well the energy invested in the existing delegation could end up being wasted if the legislators were no longer in office following the special election.

Despite all of its careful efforts, even Disney could not plan for decisions by the United States Supreme Court. Nor could the company plan for a major surprise when Miami Mayor Bob High defeated Governor Burns during the April 1966 Democratic primary election. Burns had been an ardent supporter of the Florida project from day one, providing logistical and political support when needed. His defeat meant replacing reliable support with an unknown. Then the November general election brought another surprise when Claude Kirk defeated Mayor High and, in doing so, became the first Republican governor of Florida since 1872.

Kirk's victory left Disney at the mercy of an unfamiliar political situation in Florida, a Republican governor and Democratic majority in the Florida House and Senate. An obvious question was whether this split would lead to legislative gridlock. If so, Disney's chances of getting its unique legislative package approved could be in danger and, with it, the entire Florida project. Yet even with these uncertainties, the company decided to move forward. Too much had been invested to nix the project based on only possible problems. However, as the political turmoil of 1966 came to a close, the project would encounter something even more disrupting: the death of its genius.

## Progressing without Walt Disney

On December 15, 1966, Walt Disney died following a brief battle with cancer. His death impacted the creative bearings of the entire project. After all, Walt had been the strategic and inspirational leader for the effort. Only weeks before his death, he had invited Billy Dial to California to meet with him and to tour Disneyland. Whether Walt suspected the meeting would be one of his final ones with a Florida official is unclear. During the visit, however, Walt assured Dial that if something were to happen to him, the Florida project would proceed under the capable direction of Roy Disney and other key executives. This assurance was prescient as, after Disney's death, Roy Disney took over the company's decision-making and vowed the Florida project would move forward. Disney biographer Bob Thomas recalled in his book Building a Company Roy's explanation of the matter:

> We're going to finish this park, and we're going to do it just the way Walt wanted it. Don't you ever forget it. I want every one of you to do just exactly what you were going to do when Walt was alive.

While Roy Disney's instructions were directed at the many creative planning and financial aspects of the Florida project currently in motion, they also meant the company would be finalizing the Reedy Creek legislative package, a goal that was completed not long after Disney's death in late 1966.

## Drafting the Legislative Bills

### The Legislation Behind Project Future, Spring 1967

Within weeks after Walt Disney's death, Helliwell was in Orlando to meet with the area's legislative delegates. His goal was to assure them that the company remained committed to the Florida project. In fact, Helliwell advised the legislative leaders that Roy Disney had personally assured him the project was on track.

The message was clear. Rather than cancel or delay Project Future, Disney was actively working on the package of legislative bills needed to establish the project. Much of the actual drafting work had been given to Helmut Furth, one of Disney's outside attorneys at the Donovan law firm. In addition to writing the actual bills, Disney also needed to identify sponsors for the legislation. For this task, it selected a well-respected State Senator named Bob Elrod to shepherd the package through the legislature.

With the 1967 session scheduled to begin in April, the company would need to complete discussions with local delegates and would need to secure their support quickly. To minimize the political posturing that often came with high-profile meetings involving Disney, the company quietly scheduled a private gathering of the local legislative delegates at the Villa Nova Restaurant in Winter Park, Florida. However, any hopes of this being the beginning of an uneventful process were shattered with news in early 1967 that the federal courts had again overturned the reapportionment results. The result was that Disney would once more have to persuade legislators, some of whom might not even be in the legislature when it came time to vote on the company's package, to support the plan. Still, the company remained undaunted. This new uncertainty became just another consequence to deal with, and the local delegation meeting went ahead as scheduled.

On February 2, 1967, Helliwell and Hawkins joined Roy Disney, Foster, and several other Disney officials at another invitation-only meeting in Winter Park, Florida. Other participants included politicians and business leaders from throughout Florida. It was here that Walt's final production, the EPCOT film outlining the Florida project, received its first viewing outside of the company. Disney had reserved Orlando's largest movie complex, the Wometco Park Theaters in Winter Park, for the elaborate event that would include a summary of the proposed legislation. The event started in the Park West Theater with the invitation-only presentation featuring various speakers and the film that explained the project in greater detail than ever before. The event then moved next door to the Park East Theater for a press conference describing the plans.

The significance of the meeting was immense. It was the first major Disney-held event related to the project in over a year, and more significantly the first since Walt Disney had passed in December 1966. Two versions of the film, known as Walt Disney's EPCOT '66, were produced for the event. One focused on government officials and the other on corporations' potential participation in the nascent project. By now, the cost of the Disney project was projected at $600 million.

More so than even the November 1965 meeting in Orlando in which Walt Disney officially announced the project, this meeting had taken on a circus atmosphere. For instance, the company arranged for a planeload of New York bankers and members of the press to fly into Orlando for the event. After arriving at the McCoy Jetport on the afternoon of February 2, the New York delegation boarded three chartered buses for the short drive to Winter Park. On the way, local economic development officials gave a brief tour of Orlando and pitched how Orlando was developing into a significant center of business and commerce in the Southeast. The efforts to use the Disney project to raise Central Florida's national profile were in full force.

The somewhat surreal nature of the event was further evidenced by Governor Kirk's grand entrance. Although Kirk had been in office for only a short time, he was widely regarded as a colorful character. Born in January 1926 near San Bernardino, California—not far from the Anaheim orange groves that became Disneyland—he had graduated from Emory University and the University of Alabama School of Law. After moving to Florida to pursue business interests, in 1964 he had unsuccessfully run as a Republican for the United States Senate. Two years later his luck changed when he defeated Mayor High and became Florida's first Republican governor since Reconstruction. His 1966 gubernatorial campaign was a high profile affair that occasionally focused more on his colorful personal life than his stances on issues. Indeed, his nickname of "Kissing Claude" during the campaign only furthered the interest of some persons in his political personality.

Kirk's high-profile arrival at the Disney event did little to change his reputation. After arriving in Orlando that morning, Kirk and several Disney officials, including Roy Disney, met for a private luncheon on the rooftop restaurant of Orlando's Langford Hotel. From there, Roy Disney and Kirk drove to Winter Park in a nine-passenger Lincoln Continental limousine adorned with flags on the front, similar to a presidential vehicle. The limousine itself was famous; it had been built originally for Joseph Kennedy, father of John F. Kennedy. The vehicle had been driven up from the Palm Beach area where Kirk kept it for various South Florida functions. A crowded group of reporters and photographers greeted the black limo complete with a siren-flashing escort by state police.

The event had all the markings of a Hollywood movie premiere, and its curious nature increased as the officials entered the theater. For instance, upon arriving, State Senate President Verle Pope could not enter the theater; he had forgotten to bring his ticket to the event. Not recognizing Pope as a Senator, security refused to admit him. Finally Senator Beth Johnson interceded on his behalf, Pope's identity was confirmed, and he was allowed to join the gathering.

Another example of the unique nature of the setting involved the appearance of a Mrs. Dorothy Austin. While Roy Disney was seated and waiting for the film, Austin approached and pecked a kiss on his cheek. The press noticed and immediately asked, "Who is this woman?" Their curiosity may have been piqued by the fact that, during Kirk's recent campaign, an unknown woman was frequently by his side. She ended up becoming his wife and serving as Florida's first lady, but the Kirk story generated great interest among the press.

Austin's kiss was of a decidedly more benign nature. As it turned out, the actual story was much less interesting than the media first thought. In addition to working for a Daytona Beach paper, Austin was Roy Disney's cousin.

Still, the nearby press asked her to again kiss Roy Disney for their cameras and she obliged. These nuances served to exacerbate the excitement surrounding the February 1967 event. The Disney project was leaving an indelible impression on Central Florida in many ways.

Once the February 2 meeting started, it took on a business-like tone. Helliwell opened the meeting and greeted the legislators and other special guests. He then introduced General Potter who in turn introduced the twenty-five-minute movie about Disney's plans for the Florida project. The imagery of the brilliant Walt Disney discussing his signature City of Tomorrow vision via film just months after his death was compelling and inspiring.

Following the EPCOT movie, Roy Disney addressed the crowd and provided even more details about Disney's commitment to the project. He also explained that Disney's master vision for the project included the world's first ever glass-domed city, Disney's City of Tomorrow. Plans called for the city to be air-conditioned with fifty acres under the glass dome. A signature of the city would be a thirty-story mixed-use hotel that would dramatically rise through the dome's roof. Although the company did not announce a construction date for the EPCOT portion of the project, Disney did suggest that the city would cost roughly $75 million and could take over twenty-five years to complete.

Donn Tatum followed Roy Disney and furnished details concerning the company's legislative package. Finally, Governor Kirk closed the presentation with another promise that Florida would provide strong support for this ground-breaking effort. He also discussed the findings from another ERA study that had been completed in 1966. In that study, ERA had focused on expected attendance and revenue the Disney World project would develop for the region and the state. One of the most significant findings was that, over the course of the first ten years, the project would generate fifty thousand new jobs and over $6.5 billion in economic impact for the state.

After the meeting concluded, the publicity effort went statewide. Roy Disney and Governor Kirk flew to Jacksonville, Florida, where they taped a television special that would be broadcast throughout the state that evening along with the EPCOT film. The company was doing everything it could to inform and to persuade Floridians that Project Future would benefit everybody.

The February event turned out to be a big success for Disney in several ways, one of the most important being expressions of support from key legislators. When it came to legislative representation, Disney was in a unique position. Seven state Senators and six state Representatives found portions of their districts within Disney's forty-three square miles of property. Roughly 8 percent of the entire Florida legislature counted some piece of Disney's land inside their district. Fortunately for Disney, Senate President Pope and House Speaker Ralph Turlington both expressed strong support for the project and its anticipated legislative package. Other legislative leaders, including many in the

Osceola and Orange County delegations, echoed Pope's and Turlington's support.

The meeting did produce one awkward political moment, though. Following his defeat in the 1966 Democratic primary, Governor Burns had implored Disney to hire him to represent the company in matters related to government relations in the state. Burns even went so far as to plan an Orlando-area office for his post-gubernatorial consulting efforts. In January 1967, Burns claimed in a newspaper interview he would be retained as a business and government consultant by Disney. Reporters at the Winter Park event asked Donn Tatum about Burns's potential hiring, and Tatum expressed the company's appreciation for the help that Burns as governor had provided but denied Disney had hired him. In fact, Burns had not even been invited to the event. Later he tried to qualify his claim. Whether it was simply a miscommunication or something more, Disney did not hire Burns though it did subsequently hire Burns's son, William Burns, to head Disney's parking and transportation efforts at the resort.

During the February visit, key Disney officials, including Roy Disney, Card Walker, Donn Tatum, and Joe Potter, took the time to tour the Project Future property. Surveying the property both by land and boat, they saw clearly that the effort to turn a swamp into a world-class amusement project, much less one that included an experimental city, would be massive. The group was convinced they would have to ramp up their development efforts if they wanted to open the resort by 1971.

At the same time, the company was increasing its lobbying efforts. Indeed, later that same week Helliwell returned to the Park West Theater for a public hearing with the legislative delegates from Osceola and Orange Counties. Joining him was Helmut Furth, the New York lawyer who counseled Disney on many decisions related to the project and who had drafted significant portions of the legislation. The attorneys discussed a wide range of issues including the scope of the proposed new cities and their powers. The legislators seemed particularly interested in how these new cities would interact with the existing county governments. According to an article in the Tampa Tribune, Helliwell assured the delegation that Disney was "not trying to set up a 'private kingdom' where no one can vote." Indeed, he suggested the company had not decided exactly who would be allowed to live in these cities. Also, he explained the company was not trying to avoid governance by the counties through the use of its new municipalities and improvement district.

This same issue arose again one month later in March 1967 when Foster and local attorney Phil Smith attended a Saturday afternoon hearing with the county delegates on the proposed legislation. The legislators asked pointed questions regarding whether Disney's municipal and improvement district framework would be exempt from county and state regulations. In particular, they seemed concerned that the forty-two square-mile property would be immune from existing taxes in Orange and Osceola Counties. Foster assured the legislators that Disney would not use legislation to obtain a unique tax advantage. In fact, according to an article in the Orlando Sentinel, he went so far as to say "[t]he use of governmental bonds (tax exempt) for building any function that could be built privately is repugnant to us."

By April 1967, the company had presented its plans to a wide variety of political, economic, and elected officials, some of whom were little known. The actual composition of the legislature was not certain until the March 1967 special election was complete. While Senator Elrod had survived the changes, two of the effort's biggest local supporters, Senators Irlo Bronson and Beth Johnson, decided not to seek re-election under the new legislative districts.

Although the legislation seemed set for success, several potential issues remained. For starters, with Kirk serving as a Republican governor, the state was in the unique position of having a governor of one party serving with a legislature controlled by the other party. In addition, the Democratic Party controlled Florida's executive cabinet. Since Democrats across the board had historically governed Florida, this new scenario at least presented the possibility of unanticipated issues.

Furthermore, Governor Kirk was increasingly known as someone who was not afraid to engage in tough politics. After taking office, he embarked on aggressive efforts to root out corruption and crime in Florida. This action caused some discomfort among the status quo. Neither was he afraid to take political shots, even sometimes veiled in good nature, at opposition party leaders. For instance, during one trip to California to meet with Disney officials, Kirk was given a tour of new Disney technology, which included a mechanical audio-animatronic ape character. Upon seeing the ape-themed machine, Kirk shook hands with the creation and quipped, "Verle Pope, I believe?" referring to the Democratic Senate President. There was no evidence that this or other events caused opposition to Disney's efforts, but the legislative package would encounter several unexpected bumps along the way.

On April 17, 1967, Disney's legislative package was officially introduced in both the Florida House and Senate. On that day, legislative leaders took the extraordinary step of interrupting pending business to show the EPCOT film in both chambers. Helliwell briefly addressed the joint gathering to explain why these unique governing structures were needed. Although unique, he said, the measures were in fact simply a logical extension of existing laws related to special districts.

Support for the Disney project seemed strong, but not long into the session two unanticipated challenges arose. Later Foster described the situation in his memoirs:

> *Things were progressing in good order, questions were answered, explanation accepted, amendments were proposed and worked out. Then a curious thing happened. Everything stopped, walking through the halls of the capital building it was as though people would say when introduced, "Disney who?"*

Word quietly reached Foster that the source of the unanticipated cold shoulder was the Florida Telephone Company and the Florida Power Company, who were apparently concerned about how Disney's establishing its own telephone and power services might affect their interests. Fortunately, after meeting with the telephone company's Orlando-based lobbyist, Tom Gurney, and attorneys from the power company, the concerns were resolved and the legislative process restarted just as quickly as it had stopped. The message was clear, though: even Disney and its massive project were subject to the existing Florida political machine and its varied interests.

Another challenge arose when the Orange County Commission filed a set of five objections to the legislation soon after it was introduced. The objections focused on the concerns that Helliwell and Foster had faced in the earlier local delegation meetings. While some concerns— for instance, requiring the new cities to pay expenses if prisoners were housed in the county jail—were minor, one of the objections could have been a significant impediment to developing the project. In particular, the Commission sought to prohibit the improvement district from building or operating hotels and motels. Clearly, this prohibition could have caused problems for Disney, because the project called for on-site guest lodging. Fortunately, the company was able to negotiate solutions to these objections and the legislation moved forward.

Within days of its introduction, the various committees and the Florida House passed the legislation 109-1 with hardly any debate. Subsequently Senator Elrod presented the legislative package to the Senate, and the legislation passed there without debate. Disney's innovative improvement district and accompanying new municipalities had now cleared their legislative hurdles. The realization of Walt's vision was increasingly close.

On May 5, 1967, the legislation was forwarded to Governor Kirk for his signature. One week later in the garden of the governor's mansion, he hosted a ceremony in which he signed the legislation. Business and political leaders from throughout the state, Roy Disney, and other Disney executives attended. Kirk's young daughter, Claudia, was present too. Whether intentional or not, her presence foreshadowed the major role Disney World would play in the lives of children.

Not wanting to understate the importance of the event, Kirk proclaimed that the bill's signing ranked in historical significance with Ponce de Leon's discovery of Florida. The official proclamation read:

When some future generation studies the history of Florida, three events may well stand out above all others: the discovery of Florida by Ponce de Leon; the magic moment when Henry Flagler brought the railroad to Palm Beach and opened South Florida for development; and the equally magic moment when Walt and Roy Disney decided to make Florida their second home. Gov. Claude Kirk. May 12, 1967.

Upon concluding his remarks, he signed the bills with a series of ceremonial pens engraved on their base with "Signing of Disney World Legislation: Claude R. Kirk Jr., Gov., May 12, 1967." Almost immediately after Kirk signed the bill, Disney's fortunes improved. The State Road Board approved a reallocation of millions of dollars in highway funds to the project's vicinity. The road improvement funds were part of a carefully orchestrated effort by Governor Kirk and his team following a meeting with Roy Disney at the Beverly Wilshire Hotel in California. Kirk and Roy Disney had discussed the company's needs to complete the project.

Since the voters had defeated the road bond issue in November 1965, Disney still needed a commitment from the State of Florida to improve access to the project. Coming less than an hour after Kirk signed Disney's legislation, the road board's vote diverted $5 million in funds over the next five years to the Disney project area. The board also adopted a new funding formula for future road projects that Disney could beneficially use for later highway improvements. Still though, the star of the day was the now-passed Disney legislative package.

The three pieces of legislation that Kirk signed represented the privatization of many traditional local regulatory responsibilities. Each enabled Walt's dream to become reality. Disney's legislative package included bills that created two new municipalities, an improvement district, and revisions to Florida's intellectual property laws. The strategy for creating the municipalities and an improvement district centered on obtaining the broadest possible governance authority. The improvement district would serve as the primary regulatory tool, one that would govern many of the typical local responsibilities of land use regulation, building codes, utility service, and the like. For regulatory areas that the improvement district could not govern, the two municipalities would step in and control.

Chapter 9 1967

# The Reedy Creek Improvement District

The legislation that created the actual Reedy Creek Improvement District is more than a hefty seventy-five pages. Even more impressive than the length is the scope of the District's authority. In a technical sense, to create the Improvement District, the Florida legislature essentially codified the May 13, 1966, Circuit Court decree that established the Reedy Creek Drainage District, and then expanded the scope of its authority. Section 9 of the legislation gives Reedy Creek many of the powers a municipality would typically possess such as the right to own property and the right to maintain a corporate seal, but it also gives several less typical powers such as the authority to exercise eminent domain outside of its jurisdictional boundaries. Other powers granted to the District include many typically held by a municipality: land reclamation, water and flood control, waste collection and disposal, pest control, fire protection, issuance of bonds, land use, and building regulations.

In several cases, the legislation empowered the District to engage in less typical acts, such as operating an airport and heliport for passenger and freight service. This authority was needed since Disney's initial vision called for a jetport of the future with his City of Tomorrow. Although the jetport was never developed, Disney did incorporate aviation history into the project when on October 17, 1971, one of the country's first short-length airstrips, known as the STOLport for Short Take-Off and Landing, debuted at the resort.

During the airstrip's short time of operation, two airlines, Shawnee and Executive, operated passenger flights from the main airports in Orlando and Tampa directly to Disney World on small passenger turboprop planes. Plans were also in place to operate twenty-minute STOL flights between Disney's property and a NASA airstrip at Cape Kennedy. The resort also maintained an Ultralight Flightpark near the EPCOT Center for private nonpassenger purposes. These landing strips were eventually abandoned, but at least one helipad remains in the nonpublic area of EPCOT, near the Living Seas Pavilion, as a legacy of the original 1967 legislation.

One of the recurrent themes of this legislation was the granting of broad powers to the District for experimental technologies. For instance, when the legislature provided the District with authority to operate transportation systems, the statutory language contemplated systems "whether now or hereafter invented or developed including without limitation novel and experimental facilities." Similarly, the legislation authorized the District to operate "new and experimental public facilities" and "new and experimental sources of power and energy." In fact, the goal of enabling the District to govern outside of conventional norms was further demonstrated by a separate section within the legislation directly on point:

> *[I]n order to promote the development and utilization of new concepts, designs and ideas in the fields of recreation and community living, the District shall have the power and authority to examine into, develop and utilize new concepts, designs and ideas, and to own, acquire, construct, reconstruct, equip, operate, maintain, extend and improve such experimental public facilities and services . . . as the Board may from time to time determine.*

Clearly, both the legislature and Disney conceived of a project that, while in many respects operated as a conventional municipality, possessed a broad scope of enabling authority to approach governance from a more novel perspective. This authority was the type that Walt himself had anticipated would be necessary to accomplish such a unique project.

For governing purposes, the legislation created a five-person Board of Supervisors, all of whom had to own land within the district and a majority of which had to be residents of Osceola, Orange, or an adjoining county. To elect the Board, the legislation provided: "each landowner shall be entitled to one (1) vote in person or by written proxy for every acre of land and for every major fraction of an acre owned by him in the District." This interesting provision meant that prospective nonlandowner residents, such as renters, or landowners owning less than one-half acre would not be entitled to vote in board elections.

In addition to establishing the Reedy Creek district, Disney sought legislative approval for two new municipalities within the district: the City of Bay Lake and the City of Reedy Creek. A review of this legislation reveals a grant of somewhat typical municipal powers. However, what is atypical is the fact that Disney essentially controlled the governance of both cities by limiting their populations to small groups of Disney employees and their families. The cities operated much like the District; that is, as a regulatory tool for governing Project Future. Indeed, many of the powers the District held were concurrently held by the two municipalities.

However, there were several interesting exceptions where the cities possessed some powers that the District did not. The exceptions included authority to:

- Issue business and professional licenses and to collect fees related to them
- Build and maintain health care facilities, including hospitals and health care research facilities

- Provide police services
- Regulate the manufacturing and sale of alcohol
- Establish and operate a municipal court, including appointment of a municipal judge and city prosecutor

Even though the legislature did not provide the District directly with these powers, both the cities' legislation and the District's legislation provided for a system by which the cities could provide these services within the unincorporated areas of the district upon agreement of the entities. The effect of the arrangement was: since the Disney controlled all of the entities, it maintained the power to provide police services, hospital services, municipal court services, and the like within the entire boundaries of the District.

Although the District elected not to offer some of these services, such as operating a police force or municipal court system, the 1967 legislative package reserved almost all local governance responsibilities for either the cities or the District. Indeed, one of the few areas of government that Disney would not obtain authority over through the legislation was a school system. The company did announce plans for a "School of Tomorrow" as part of its City of Tomorrow project, but it repeatedly assured local and state authorities that it had no intention of operating a school system. Indeed, at the 1967 Winter Park event, the company had said it would not operate an entire school system. Instead, it would provide support for experimental school programs within the existing school frameworks.

The uniquely broad scope of Reedy Creek's authority would soon be tested within the Florida courts to determine whether the District and the cities, novel as they were, comported with the requirements of Florida's constitution.

### Encountering Legal Problems for the Build Out, 1968

After the legislation's passage, Disney's project planning accelerated rapidly toward a planned 1971 opening. In early 1968, though, a nonlegislative front presented a new challenge, a strike by the Local 673 of the International Union of Operating Engineers. The striking workers focused their demands on higher pay and improved work conditions at the massive site. By mid-January 1968, the Orlando Sentinel was reporting that the strike had resulted in violence between union and nonunion workers:

> . . . [m]ore than 20 nonunion construction workers were marched military style from the west side of the 27,400 Disney Word plot . . . by 300 union members who roughed up one man. The nonunion workers were forced to chant: "The union wins. We won't be back again" as they walked off.

While this type of incident could have easily raised red flags within the Disney group, according to personnel in Governor Kirk's office, company officials had anticipated the strike and remained committed to the Disney project during the process.

That commitment was further tested on February 13, 1968, when state and local union leaders organized an anti-Disney rally at Orlando's Tangerine Bowl. Organizers had predicted a crowd of twenty to fifty thousand, but the final count was only six thousand or so. As the forty-five minute rally ended, the organizers attempted one last bit of drama. They invited all attendees to the Disney project site where presumably they would not be simply visiting for fun. However, even this effort fell flat. Law enforcement personnel reported that few members of the rally crowd bothered to make the twenty-three-mile ride from the Tangerine Bowl to the Disney site.

It was hardly a surprise then when on Friday, February 16, Disney and union officials announced an end to the thirty-two day strike with the parties reaching an interim pact on wages and other benefits. The union problem had been solved. Yet an even graver challenge was brewing for Project Future, one that would determine whether the project's very existence would survive legal scrutiny before the Florida Supreme Court.

Chapter 10 1968-1969

# Lawsuit Challenges

By November 1968, Project Future was facing a threshold legal challenge: Would the Florida Supreme Court uphold the constitutionality of Disney's unique form of improvement district governance?

The case of State of Florida v. Reedy Creek Improvement District[1] centered on the propriety of allowing the Reedy Creek Improvement District to issue drainage bonds as part of the overall project development. The bond revenue would be used to drain and to reclaim submerged land within the district. The maturity dates for the bonds ranged from 1970 until 2004.

The lawsuit represented a somewhat odd procedural situation. The State, which had previously created the

District through the 1967 legislation, was challenging the very scope of authority that had been granted to the District. The exercise was an important one, though, for it provided an opportunity for all of the parties to essentially test the legality of the District's unique structure within the Florida courts.

Technically, Reedy Creek filed the lawsuit against the State of Florida and property owners and citizens within the District. In that sense, Disney, as the force behind the District, was suing itself as owner of most of the property in the District. Prior to filing the lawsuit, Disney had divided the District into two distinct areas, Subdistrict One and Subdistrict Two, via a resolution adopted by the District's Board of Supervisors on January 31, 1968. Following this division, Disney instructed their engineers at Gee & Jensen to begin focusing on the area encompassed by Subdistrict One.

By May of that year, the District's Board, which General Potter now headed, adopted a resolution to authorize use of the bond authority the 1967 legislation had provided. In particular, the Board approved drainage revenue bonds not to exceed $12 million for Subdistrict One. There was a problem, though. Before Disney could realistically market the bonds, it needed to determine whether the unique bonding authority that the legislature had given the District was in fact legal under Florida's Constitution. Therefore, Disney decided to file suit to ultimately bring the matter before the Florida Supreme Court for a final ruling.

Soon thereafter, the State answered Disney's complaint and provided several reasons why the bonds were not permissible. However, this opposition was clearly more staged than real, for the entire lawsuit was premised on testing the constitutionality of the District's bond authority rather than affirmatively seeking to oppose that authority. After all, had the latter been the case, the State would have likely filed suit within the year after the legislation was adopted in May 1967, but it did not.

On June 15, 1968, the state's attorney, Arthur Stead, appeared before Judge Murray W. Overstreet of Florida's Ninth Judicial Circuit for a hearing on the matter. Tom DeWolf of the Helliwell firm represented the District. To open the hearing, DeWolf called Phil Smith, a fellow outside attorney and a current District Board member, to testify. Other than Disney, Smith was one of the few individual landowners within the District. During his testimony, Smith explained that the proposed bonds would be for work comprising roughly one thousand of the District's twenty-seven thousand. He also testified that without these bonds, the land could not be reclaimed for development use.

The testimony of another board member, J.J. Griffin, Jr., followed. Griffin was a former State Representative whose district had included Disney property. While in the legislature, Griffin had chaired the powerful House Appropriations Committee. He testified that the land within Subdistrict One was essentially useless for development purposes unless it was drained and unless water controls were put in place.

DeWolf's next witness, Hubert Gee of the Gee & Jensen firm, confirmed the importance of drainage and water control from an engineer's professional perspective. To support his testimony, Gee relied on a report from April 1968 that his firm had prepared for the District. Entitled "Special Report on Water Control for the Reedy Creek Improvement District," the study had provided several interesting findings that further evidenced the unlikely fact that Disney would select these parcels on which to build a massive resort complex. In particular, the report noted that a major part of Disney's twenty-seven thousand acres was below the elevation of the surrounding land and surplus waters, meaning much of the adjacent land would drain onto the Disney property. Indeed, water in the area typically traveled through Bonnet Creek and Reedy Creek, both flowing onto Disney property, and then into the Reedy Creek swamp, which drained into the Kissimmee River system.

These large volumes of water could inundate the land if controls were not put in place. This made the Osceola County portion of the property, much of which included the large tract that Disney had purchased from Senator Irlo Bronson, even more important, because much of the water flowed into that area. In fact, later Reedy Creek administrator Ray Maxwell later referred to the Osceola portion as "the district's kidney" when describing the importance that this less-developed property played in the overall drainage scheme for the area.

As the project's Chief Consulting Engineer, Gee's testimony was important because it provided a technical explanation of how the drainage bonds would benefit the larger area surrounding the Disney property as opposed to benefiting only the Disney parcel. His testimony was not without its own curiosity, though. Indeed, if there remained any question about whether the State and Disney had coordinated efforts in the lawsuit, the question was likely resolved during Gee's cross-examination during which the state's attorney elicited some of the most favorable testimony yet related to the importance of the bond authority. The testimony, in favor of Disney, was an unlikely result from the so-called opposing counsel.

To conclude his portion of the hearing, DeWolf briefly examined E. Carlton Heeseler, an investment banker with the New York firm Kidder and Peabody. Heeseler testified that in his professional opinion the proposed drainage bonds were indeed marketable and that using bonds in this manner was an increasingly prevalent practice in other parts of the United States. Following Heeseler's testimony, the Disney attorneys rested their case.

One final bit of curious legal maneuvering remained, though. Judge Overstreet asked the state's attorney if he wanted to present any argument on the State's behalf. The attorney, either completely flummoxed or, more likely, understanding his scripted role in the matter, meekly responded, "Yes, sir, but I don't know what to say."

With that, the hearing concluded and the trial judge promptly ruled in Disney's favor. However, to get the matter before the Florida Supreme Court and to obtain a definitive ruling on the constitutionality of the District, the parties needed to continue their adversarial charade a little bit longer. On June 28, the State formally appealed Judge Overstreet's ruling to Florida's high court.

On July 22, the State filed its brief on appeal, and only two days later the District filed its response brief—a remarkably short turn-around time and yet another fact that seemed to indicate coordination between the District and the State in the matter. In the response brief, Reedy Creek argued that rather than merely benefiting a private company with private interests, the unique nature of the district should be upheld, for it served to benefit the State of Florida as a whole.

In support of this contention, Reedy Creek pointed out that an estimated 19,500,000 additional tourists would come to Florida during the project's first ten years of operation. Reedy Creek and Disney also estimated that the project would result in over $6 billion in new spending and would result in new state tax revenues exceeding $240 million. In addition, the response brief asserted that no public funds would be used to construct the massive project. All in all, the gist of the argument was that while Disney might benefit from the district's unique format, the State of Florida and its citizens would also realize a great boon in revenue, jobs, and tax receipts.

Ultimately, the Florida Supreme Court upheld not only the trial court's validation of the drainage bonds but also the very structure of the district itself. In doing so, the

Court found the State's challenges to be "untenable." For instance, it disposed of the State's first argument that the bonds represented an unlawful issuance of public funds for a private purpose by noting that "the promotion and development of tourism and recreation" serve as "valid public purposes" as determined both by the state legislature and affirmed by numerous Florida cases. On this point, the court held:

> *Successful completion and operation of the District no doubt will greatly aid the Disney interest and its contemplated Disneyworld project. However, it is obvious that to a lesser degree the contemplated benefits of the District will inure to numerous inhabitants of the District in addition to persons in the Disney complex.*

The duality of this benefit persuaded the Court that the bond issuance would achieve the level of advancing a general public purpose within the state. Of course, one might note that the Court's holding was based in part on "inhabitants" ultimately residing in the district, something that would actually never materialize beyond a handful of company employees and their families.

Would this fact have altered the Court's opinion had it known? Obviously any answer is founded on speculation. However, in this instance, the Court's emphasis on the project's extensive tourism benefits seem to indicate that even without residents, the District's activities would have risen to the level of a "public purpose." Indeed, the Court itself noted that "the integrated plan or workings of the District are essentially and primarily directed toward encouraging and developing tourism" for both residents and nonresidents of the state.

The Court next dealt with the State's threshold argument that the District's enabling act was a "mere subterfuge" to avoid creating a new municipality. The gist of this contention was that by creating a unique "multi-county, multi-purpose" special district, the legislature developed a form of governance unlike anything ever before, with the State apparently suggesting that doing so violated the Florida Constitution. The Court agreed that the District was a unique vehicle for governing. However, uniqueness alone is not a fatal flaw as long as it does not violate constitutional parameters. In this case, the Court concluded:

So long as specific constitutional provisions are not offended, the Legislature in the exercise of its plenary authority may create a special improvement district encompassing more than one county and possessing multi-purpose powers essential to the realization of a valid public purpose.

Finally, the Court disposed of several additional arguments related to the technical nature of how the District was created and the scope of its authority, in each instance finding the State's arguments unpersuasive. With that, the legality of the legislature's experiment in bestowing public governance powers upon a private entity was affirmed.

With this holding, the years of legal and regulatory planning that ultimately produced the Reedy Creek Improvement District had been validated. The legality of Project Future's expansive, multi-purpose special district was now official.

## Opposing the Florida Ranch Lands Lawsuit

The legal challenges facing Disney's Florida project in 1968 were not limited to the Florida Supreme Court matter. Indeed, Disney's legal bills for the year were likely much higher than normal, for it also faced a civil lawsuit filed by Florida Ranch Lands alleging fraud by Disney and ERA. In a complaint filed on August 5, 1968, FRL sued for damages that it claimed to have suffered in the form of lost real estate commissions. The allegations dated back to William Lund's original trip for ERA in December 1963 to investigate potential sites for Project Future. Disney's instructions to Price, Lund, and ERA regarding the importance of keeping Disney's and their identity secret were clear to all.

However, apparently the instructions regarding how Lund was to conduct his investigation were not as clear. During his visits to Florida, Lund had met with Florida Ranch Lands' personnel as part of his disguised role on behalf of a New York investment group looking for property in the Sunshine State. The lawsuit claimed that during these visits and related conversations between Lund and Florida Ranch Lands, Disney had first become aware of the Demetree, Bay Lake, and Hamrick parcels that would later comprise a significant portion of the Disney project. FRL alleged that Lund took the information they had provided and given it to Disney, who then purchased the Demetree property without paying a commission to FRL for its work.

The facts surrounding the suit were complexly intertwined with Disney's secrecy efforts. For instance, when initially dealing with Lund in late 1963, FRL had not realized he represented Disney's interests because of the company's use of the Burke & Burke law firm in New York as a drop box for Lund's correspondence and phone conversations with FRL. As a result, when its dealings with Lund ended in March 1964, FRL did not realize that its subsequent conversations about the Demetree, Bay Lake, and Hamrick tracts in the spring of 1964 with Hawkins and Foster concerned the same interests. That Disney also concealed Foster's true identity from FRL by introducing him to the company as Bob Price from Kansas City, Missouri, had exacerbated the confusion.

In the interim, Hawkins had hired, with Disney's permission, FRL to assist him with obtaining property options in the Summer of 1964. In part this was because the company held nonexclusive listings for the two tracts. In exchange, Hawkins had agreed to split his commission on the Bay Lake and Hamrick parcels with FRL. The larger and more costly Demetree tract was excluded from the agreement, something the lawsuit alleged was fraudulent in that FRL first introduced Disney to the land through Lund.

In October 1965, FRL, like the rest of the world, officially learned the mystery company behind these purchases was Disney. Before that, though, FRL personnel such as

Nusbickel and Nelson Boice, the firm's head, were fairly certain Disney was their mystery client. A key clue had come during a visit by Disney representatives that summer. When they arrived, Hawkins arranged for Jim Morgan of FRL to give the group a boat tour of Bay Lake. The group had taken great care to not use their real names. However, one of the visitors referred to another one as "Skipper," and Morgan noticed Skipper had the initials J.F. on his jacket.

After finishing up the tour, Morgan engaged in a little amateur detective work. He thought he had seen a picture of "Skipper" in a magazine, so he started paging through old magazines he had saved and discovered a picture of Admiral Joe Fowler, who was identified in the picture's caption as an engineer for Disney. Clearly, the Skipper with the initials J.F. was Disney's Joe Fowler. Morgan had broken the code.

However, after discussing it with his FRL colleagues, they agreed it was in their company's and their client's best interest to keep the secret.[2] Also, it had appeared to be in their individual interests, for Morgan himself quickly purchased property around the Disney site before the announcement about Project Future became public. Ultimately Morgan netted more than $1 million in profit.

About this time, FRL had learned that Bob Price from Kansas City was actually Robert Price Foster, a vice president with Disney. However, not until January 1966 did FRL learn William Lund was an employee of ERA working under contract with Disney during his late 1963 visits.

FRL had discovered the connection through a series of chance events. For starters, in late October 1965, Helliwell, Hawkins, and a group of Disney officials joined Nusbickel and other FRL personnel for dinner at the University Club in Orlando. Now that Disney's role as the mystery company was official, the parties reminisced on recent events. During dinner Nusbickel casually asked Foster if he had ever heard of William Lund. Foster replied that Lund had worked with the Stanford Research Institute and had done some consulting for Disney.

Then, after the November 1965 Disney announcement, Nusbickel noticed an article in Parade Magazine that discussed the story of how Disney had selected the Central Florida site. Part of the story recounted how Disney had used the Stanford Research Institute to assist in the project. Although the account was inaccurate—Disney used Buzz Price's ERA—the mention of the Stanford firm jogged Nusbickel's memory as to his first meeting with Lund in late 1963 when Lund had told Nusbickel that he once worked for Stanford Research.

Finally, in January 1966 FRL employee Bosserman had joined a group of Florida county commissioners and planners on a trip to Anaheim, California. During the plane ride, Bosserman noticed that one of the officials had a document listing William Lund as an executive with ERA. Bosserman himself remembered Lund's name from the 1963 visit. As it turns out, Lund was presenting at the conference the group was attending. Following the session, Bosserman introduced himself to Lund. Without prompting, Lund asked Bosserman to pass along a greeting to David Nusbickel and to express Lund's regret that they were unable to work together on the Florida effort.

After discussing the matter internally, the FRL group concluded that the information provided to Lund during his visit in 1963—information that included the Demetree, Bay Lake, and Hamrick tracts—had been passed along to Disney to avoid paying FRL a full commission on the three parcels that Disney later acquired. Nelson Boice, FRL's head, decided the matter was serious enough and the money owed to FRL was large enough that a call to Roy Hawkins was necessary.

Boice called Hawkins and explained that he needed to meet with Helliwell about the commissions his company was owed on the Hamrick, Demetree, and Bay Lake tracts, and Hawkins arranged for the meeting. Soon after, Boice and his attorney traveled to Helliwell's Miami law office. Despite Boice's previous relationship with Hawkins and Helliwell, almost as soon as they arrived Helliwell told Boice that Disney did not want him to discuss the matter. Basically Boice and his attorney had traveled to Miami to say nothing more than hello. To Boice, this meant that Disney had no intention of resolving the matter amicably.

After the failed meeting in Miami, Florida Ranch Lands hired Harris Dittmar, a well-respected litigator, and sued both Disney and ERA. The suit alleged that Disney and ERA owed FRL $200,000 in unpaid commission for the Demetree tract and over $40,000 in commissions for the Bay Lake and

Hamrick tracts. On August 20, 1968, Walt Disney Productions moved to dismiss the complaint for failure to allege a proper claim. The Court disagreed with Disney, though, and on October 16, 1998, denied the dismissal motion. This denial propelled the case forward with all of the parties aggressively pursuing its claims through depositions and written discovery. For its part, Disney answered and denied FRL's complaint on December 17, 1968.

Disney's defense was based on several points. First, it claimed that its November 1963 agreement with ERA did not authorize Lund to do anything more than informally investigate large land transactions in Florida. His efforts in engaging FRL to identify actual parcels, pricing, and availability exceeded the scope of ERA's agreement with Disney. As a result, the company was not responsible for Lund's unapproved conduct. Disney also argued that regardless of Lund's unauthorized actions, it never used or even received any information regarding the Demetree, Bay Lake, and Hamrick tracts from Lund or from Florida Ranch Lands via Lund.

Disney's answer to the lawsuit also seemed to anticipate that its subterfuge related to Lund and Foster's true identity might become an issue. As a result, it claimed that these practices, though deceptive, were not fraudulent; they had been done in accordance with the Securities Exchange Act. In particular, the company claimed that because it was a public corporation, the Act allowed it to withhold the true identities of Foster and Lund to protect its shareholders from increased financial costs the company would have likely realized had its true identity been known during the land acquisition process. In essence, Disney was claiming that its deception related to Foster and Lund was done in compliance with federal law.

With the parties increasingly entrenched in their positions, a slew of Disney, ERA, and Florida Ranch Lands officials were deposed over the next several months. They included Helliwell, Hawkins, the Demetrees, Nusbickel with FRL, and both Lund and Buzz Price from ERA. The wide-ranging and sometimes contentious depositions did not appear to move the parties any closer to a settlement. Therefore, George Young, the presiding federal court judge, set the case for trial on June 9, 1969, before a jury in Orlando.

Before a jury could rule on the matter, however, the parties reached a confidential settlement that summer with all parties dismissing their claims and defenses. The lawsuit was finished, but the fact that it was filed in the first place yet again represented the difficult balance Disney faced in guarding its secrecy while also accumulating tens of thousands of acres of land for Project Future.

The lawsuit also seemed to distance ERA and Disney. By this time, Walt Disney, who had encouraged Price to start ERA in the first place, had died, leaving ERA without its strongest advocate in the company. In addition, remaining Disney officials were indignant that Lund caused the entire lawsuit by acting outside the scope of Disney's November 1963 agreement with ERA. Although ERA continued to do

some work for Disney, Price ultimately sold the company
and found himself outside of the company's inner circle as
it prepared to build Project Future.

## Unveiling the World, 1969

With the Florida Supreme Court lawsuit over, Disney
was now ready to move toward completing the massive
project, which included identifying key participants to build
the massive resort. For starters, the company announced on
February 11, 1969, that Allen Contracting Company had
signed a three-year agreement to serve as general contractor.
Disney also announced that it had entered into an agreement
with Bank of America and seven banks from Florida for a
$50 million credit line to advance construction.

Then on April 30, 1969, Disney returned to its habit of
holding large political and press gatherings to announce
significant aspects of the project. In this case, the company
used a four-day event in Orlando to unveil large models,
a seventeen-minute overview film, and renderings for the
resort. Governor Kirk joined the Disney contingency for the
event in which the company announced that a series of major
U.S. corporations would be participating in construction of
the project. These included well-known companies such as
U.S. Steel, RCA, and Monsanto.

While the project was quickly nearing its October 1971
opening date, the April 1969 meeting revealed several major
unsettled details. For instance, officials with the project were
still referring to the planned Polynesian resort as a twelve-

story building when in fact the final version of the resort would be a series of two- and three-story structures. The company also continued to discuss building Asian, Venetian, and Persian themed resorts around the central lagoon, three projects that would never end up being built.

The discrepancies also applied to the project's first theme park, the Magic Kingdom. In terms of the Magic Kingdom, the April 1969 plans included several major features that also would not be constructed. These included a Thunder Mesa area that would feature a major new dark ride known as the Western River Expedition, an attraction that would rival the scale of Disneyland's popular Pirates of the Caribbean. Despite these unrealized features, the plans the company unveiled at that April event included most of what Disney World guests would have found on opening day.

With the close of the April 1969 conference, a chapter in the history of Project Future also closed. Roughly six years after first focusing on Central Florida, Disney was now well on its way toward completing the Walt Disney World Resort. Project Future, first conceived in the early 1960s, was now quickly moving from a grand concept to an equally grand reality. It would soon become an entertainment project whose long-term impact would fundamentally change the State of Florida.

Chapter 11

# The Impact of Project Future

Disney could have created amusement parks and an innovative mixed-use development without resorting to court-approved drainage districts and newly-enabled cities and improvement districts, but it chose not to do so. The choice leads to the important question, why opt for such a complex and novel approach toward developing the Florida project when other large private developments, including Disneyland, had succeeded without such a unique regulatory framework?

The answer is multifaceted and complex but clearly centers on the issue of legal control over the physical and regulatory environment that would shape the massive project. Unfortunately, the term "control," especially in a land development context, often sparks a visceral reaction centered on the idea of a big brother-like entity wildly exercising oppressive powers. Even if the response is not that strong, the idea of assigning governing powers to a private entity still may give some pause.

Increased private control over governance is not itself an inherent danger. Rather, it is the granting of that control to a potentially abusive entity that can result in problems. In the case of Disney in the 1960s, the Florida legislature had little reason to question the motives of the company's request. In fact, Disney's reasoning for the request demonstrated otherwise. For instance, when it developed Disneyland, the company failed to acquire much of the surrounding land. As the project became popular, a slew of cheap motels and shops built up around the theme park, creating a visual blight, an especially troubling problem because Disney had invested so much into the appearance of Disneyland.

Therefore, it was hardly surprising that Disney feared a similar result in Florida if the project were developed without the buffer Disneyland lacked. Indeed, this fear turned out to be well founded, for the Florida project was soon surrounded by less immersive commercial developments. The difference in Florida was that the company had enough buffer land to keep those businesses away from its project.

While the buffer alone might have been sufficient to keep away undesirable businesses, it did not empower Disney to make final development decisions related to the property and the company's desire to utilize innovation in building out the project. If Disney had proceeded under the existing structures of governance, those decisions would have remained in the hands of county commissioners, building departments, fire chiefs, and other regulators. The net effect would have been to saddle Disney's progressive visions of new building techniques, water management, and land uses with the decidedly conventional regulations of what were at the time relatively undeveloped counties in Central Florida. Quite simply, it is unlikely the existing counties would have had the personnel and financial resources to govern such a massive and complex project.

Another factor in the issue of control was that Walt reached his creative and most influential apex at the same time disorder was disrupting American cities. The 1960s were a time of urban upheaval and distress, with riots and crime disrupting the nation. Walt seemed intent on countering these problems. Rather than seeking to impose order on existing institutions, he sought to create new institutions to further his goal. In doing so, he implicitly recognized the national flux of the 1960s was not something he had to destroy. He did not seem intent to force his ideals on the public as a whole. Rather, he sought increased control over a project that would never have existed but for his investment in the effort. The result was the multibillion-dollar Project Future for which Disney ultimately sought very little public funding.

The improvement district format furthered Disney's efforts to maintain control over key governance aspects of the project. However, the appropriateness of this approach is obviously not measured merely by how it benefited a private corporation like Disney. Since it acquired many of the regulatory powers that the counties would have otherwise maintained, a complete analysis of Project Future also requires consideration of how the regulatory arrangement affected state and local interests outside of Disney.

The Florida legislature's decision to create the District demonstrated a willingness to engage in novel regulatory strategies to secure the Disney project. This action leads to another important question: Was the legislature's decision to privatize much of the governing authority within Reedy Creek a wise one? To fully answer the question, one must first consider the state of rural Orange and Osceola Counties prior to Disney's Florida project. This gives context to the massive change the project would bring.

The first issue is whether the large-scale development of the area was inevitable or whether it was uniquely provoked by the Disney effort. If the answer is the former, then Disney's effect in the region is not nearly as significant as if the latter were true; if Disney had not developed, it would have been someone else. However, if the answer is the latter—that the development was uniquely provoked by Disney—then there is little doubt that the Disney project caused a massive change in this area that otherwise would not have occurred. As one commentator explained:

> That area had fewer than 370,000
> residents then, and they were making their
> unremarkable living mainly from the land—
> raising cattle, growing oranges, building

*small subdivisions. A few folks were selling pecan logs and painted coconut heads to the tourists passing on their way to beaches east and west. Maybe those visitors would detour to play golf or take photos of the water-skiing acts and lovely flowers at Cypress Gardens, but they didn't have much reason to make Orlando their destination.*

True, lots of folks were continuing the trend begun after World War II of moving to Florida for jobs or retirement. But the flat, swampy landscape of Central Florida lacked the allure of its coastline.

Of course, the mere fact that the endeavor brought significant change of an unanticipated scale does not necessarily mean the region and state benefited from the change. However, in this instance, both historical and contemporary research reveals that the Disney effort served as a boon to both the state and local economies.

## Revisiting Economic Impact

### The 1967 Findings of ERA

In 1965, the East Central Florida Regional Planning Council, which includes among its members both Orange and Osceola Counties, produced a detailed report on the regional economy and development. The report outlined some seemingly incongruous results. For instance, while it touted that the region's economy "underwent one of the most rapid and drastic changes [between 1950 and 1963] ever to take place in a U.S. region in peacetime," the report also noted that the region "contributed significantly" to Florida's overall nation-leading mortgage defaults.

The fact that the Council offered its analysis for this robustly conflicted economy in May 1965 is interesting in that, though little known to the Council, one of the largest economic forces ever to shape the region was just months from being officially announced. Indeed, the November 1965 announcement of Disney's Florida project would add a significant new variable to the area's economy and development.

To help quantify this variable, Disney commissioned a study from ERA in January 1967 that focused on the prospective economic impact that the Disney project would generate for the state and Central Florida. The report concluded that, from the start of construction through the first decade of operation, the project would generate more than $6.6 billion in "new wealth." In particular, the report estimated new visitor expenditures exceeding $3.9 billion, new payrolls reaching $2.2 billion, and more than $400 million in construction-related expenditures.

The study also estimated that the state government would realize $243 million in sales tax receipts from new visitors and new residents resulting from the project, while local governments would obtain more than $100 million in additional tax revenues. Ultimately, the report concluded that the estimated 19.5 million additional visitors coming to the Disney project in the first ten years would make a significant impact on the entire state.

The clear result was that ERA anticipated a major net gain for both the state and local governments and an opportunity for Florida to define itself broadly in terms of tourist attractions. For instance, according to the 1967 ERA report, "In 1965 only 8 percent of all activities which visitors looked forward to on a trip to Florida consisted of commercial attractions." This low number likely resulted from the state's primary attraction as a destination for beach vacations. Adding a nonbeach tourist option of Disney's magnitude would provide a compelling reason to visit Florida for those vacationers not interested in a beach trip.

The extension of these benefits to the local communities and the state as a whole was seconded by state officials such as the East Central Florida Regional Planning Council, which subsequently predicted that because of the project, "there would be a $500-million investment in tourist-related activities outside of Disney World by 1980 and a need for twenty-seven thousand more hotel and motel rooms, and seventy thousand new jobs. We see all this investment transforming tourism in Florida."

Moreover, the mere announcement of the project increased area land values more than 30 percent. In addition, even before construction was completed, all Disney World convention dates for 1972, the first year on-property conventions would start in earnest, were booked in advance, yet another indication that ERA's prediction of

Disney's economic success was well supported. Indeed, by 1972, Disney World's first full year of operation, the area's unemployment rate was 2 percent lower than the national average and the area's tax receipts, construction projects, and bank deposits had reached all-time highs. Clearly, the massive Disney project was bearing fruit for the region.

## The 1983 Disney World Effect Study

The early positive effects of the project would be revisited a decade later in another economic impact study. In 1983, Rollins College in Orlando produced a study entitled "The Disney World Effect," which used statistical data to analyze the impact of the resort on the State of Florida. The report used government statistics to reach several important conclusions related to the time period from 1970 to 1980, roughly the first decade of Disney World's operation.

In 1980, the United States population growth rate was 11 percent while Florida's rate was 43.55 percent and the three-county area surrounding Disney World was even higher at 54.45 percent.

The travel patterns of vacationers to Florida had changed dramatically. Whereas many once traveled to Florida for its beaches, by the 1980s Disney World accounted for roughly 40 percent of Florida vacationers. The counties of Orange and Osceola received the lion's share of these new guests. Tourist arrivals from 1970 to 1981 increased 648.3 percent while statewide the increase was 46.1 percent.

With the increased tourists came increased spending. Indeed, during this time frame, the entire state realized a 141.6 percent growth in guest expenditures while the three-county Orlando area experienced a 188.8 percent increase.

State expenditures in response to the growth varied widely, with education spending increasing while highway spending lagged behind. "[T]he state of Florida, with priority placed on public protection, has tried to maintain the quality of life, without great expense to the taxpayer."

Ultimately, the study concluded the following:

> The development of Disney World has served as a learning aid for the central Florida area, illustrating how radically the establishment of one industry can change an area's growth, and also, how important effective community planning is. The area has succeeded in dealing with the rapid changes and has thus served, with Disney World, to enhance Florida's attractiveness as a vacation destination for tourists, while maintaining the quality of living for the growing number of Florida residents.

From the 1983 study, it became increasingly clear that ten years into the project, both Florida and the Orlando metro area were realizing the positive impacts projected in the 1967 ERA study. That is, of course, not to say that negative impacts did not exist. Indeed, the aforementioned transportation problem highlighted just the opposite.

However, those negative effects continued to be outweighed by positive effects as the project wrapped up its first decade of operation.

Nearly twenty years later, another economic impact study would conclude that the state and region were still realizing positive impacts from the unique structure of Project Future.

## The 2004 Fishkind Study

In 2004 a study by Dr. Hank Fishkind & Associates concluded that Reedy Creek and Disney World continued to generate positive economic results. The report revealed that Disney paid over $475 million in taxes, making it Central Florida's largest taxpayer. It also found that the company paid roughly $75 million in ad valorem taxes to Orange County, an amount larger than the combined total of the next ten largest taxpayers in the county. Other significant findings include the following:

The company's annual $5.1 billion gross fiscal output in Central Florida equaled more than 8 percent of the region's total output.

The company maintained a $1.3 billion annual payroll while it fostered over $1.5 billion in other direct and indirect payroll earnings for workers in the region.

The company's total amount of paid or collected state taxes and local resort taxes exceeded $390 million.

Ultimately, the study concluded the following:

> *All of these economic activities, combined with guest and employee spending locally, provide a huge fiscal surplus of $350 million annually–$295 million per year in Orange County; $52 million per year in Osceola County; and more than $1 million per year in Brevard County. These surpluses result in a major reduction in the per year tax burden that residents otherwise would be compelled to pay for services.*[1]

The result was that over the course of three decades, Project Future continued to provide direct and indirect benefits to the local and state economies in a proportion that outweighed its negative impacts.

# Looking at Additional Impacts

## Financial

Beyond specific studies and reports, Project Future has benefited the Orlando metropolitan area in other ways. Indeed, as early as in 1970, "Disney World spawn[ed] a need for business and financial services" in greater Orlando. This included large new bank branches, financial service institutions, and insurance interests, such as a new nineteen-story building for CAN Financial Corporation and a $4.5 million headquarters for The Hartford Insurance Group.

## Environmental

The benefits derived from the creation of the District were not limited to only financial matters, though. One complaint about Reedy Creek was that its approach to development harmed the environment. Most of the criticism centers on Disney World's effect on the existing ecosystem, particular concern being directed toward Disney's treatment of wetlands. But an independent case study concluded the environmental management systems for Disney World and Reedy Creek were effectively managed and operated. Indeed, both facilities earned awards for extensive environmental accomplishments in a wide range of areas including natural resource management, pest control, water and energy conversation, and recycling. Moreover, multiple Disney hotels within the district have received the Florida Department of Environmental Protection's "Green Lodging Certification," a voluntary state program designed to "encourag[e] hotels and motels to adopt cost-saving 'green' practices that reduce waste and conserve natural resources."

Despite the unique governance structure, Disney World continues to comply with, if not exceed, environmental practices, a strong indication that the public-private dichotomy at work in the district has not led to standards lower than those if Disney World were regulated under a more traditional form of governance. The high standards may be due in part to extensive federal, regional, and state environmental regulation in the area from authorities such as the United States Environmental Protection Agency, Army Corps of Engineers, U.S. Fish and Wildlife Service,

Florida Department of Environmental Protection, and the South Florida Water Management District. In each case, the District must comply with the regulations from these entities.

In the mid-1960s, Disney entered into a U.S. Geological Survey cooperative program designed "to monitor the quantity and quality of surface and ground water in and adjacent to the [district] as an aid in the continuing management of the [district]'s water resources, and in evaluating the effects of urban activities on the hydrologic system." The effect is that the environmental practices within the district have historically been regulated by a wide variety of state and federal agencies in addition to internal District regulations.

Moreover, as early as 1971, the National Wildlife Federation recognized the Reedy Creek project "contains many innovations designed to solve a host of current environmental problems." These included the following:

- Seventeen dams and an extensive dike system to protect the project's conservation area
- A compressed-air trash removal system that delivered trash to a central management area
- A storm water and waste water system developed in conjunction with University of Florida experts designed to "render sewage harmless and even profitable"
- Power generation techniques designed to reduce thermal pollution

- Alternative pest control methods designed to limit the use of certain chemicals

These efforts led the group to conclude that "Walt Disney's successors have done just about everything that time, talent, good will and money can provide to nurture the high hopes their late boss had for Disney World."

Of course, this is not to say that environmental concerns were nonexistent. Indeed, at the time, several specific concerns included increases in traffic, loss of plant life, and negative impacts upon area citrus groves and the water supply. However, while the development has certainly affected the area, if for no reason other than sheer size, the resulting impact has not generated the negative impacts some persons predicted—especially when one considers the most realized problem, increased traffic congestion, may have been affected by the Florida project but was also attributable to interstate, turnpike, and other road construction planned before the project was even announced much less opened.

## District Governance

One final note remains pertinent to this discussion: Had the Florida state legislature believed that the District was not governing in an effective manner, it could have repealed the District's authority at any time and reassigned it to existing governance entities like Orange and Osceola Counties. Indeed, in several instances, the state legislature chose to do the exact opposite, deciding to specifically exempt the District from additional governance by those local general-purpose bodies.

For example, when the state legislature passed a law, which provided that "[e]ach independent special district shall submit to each local general-purpose government in which it is located a public facilities report and an annual notice of any changes," it specifically excluded the District from this requirement. Similarly, when the state legislature passed a law requiring local governments to prepare comprehensive plans for future growth and development, the legislature assigned this responsibility directly to the District "for the total area under its jurisdiction" instead of giving Orange and Osceola Counties authority over property within the district.

A cynical observer may suggest that these exceptions resulted from Disney's strong lobbying power within the state, but there is no evidence that any untoward influence was ever exerted to obtain these provisions. The reality is that when confronted with subsequent opportunities to reduce or expand the scope of the District's governance authority, the state legislature opted for the latter.

The legislature again turned its attention to the District's unique governance authority in February 2004 when the Comcast Corporation commenced efforts to acquire Disney, including its Florida properties. Comcast's efforts were ultimately unsuccessful, but the state legislature commissioned a report on the effects that a change in ownership might have.

The December 2004 report by the State's Office of Program Policy Analysis & Government Accountability

(OPPAGA) concludes that "in general, current accountability mechanisms are sufficient to ensure that if primary landownership changed, [the District] would continue to meet the public purpose expressed in its special act and in other legislation." This conclusion followed a review of the District's existing laws and regulations as well as consideration that the District was also subject to additional layers of governance by a variety of other state and federal agencies ranging from the U.S. Environmental Protection Agency to the South Florida Water Management District. The report determined that "[t]hese agencies provide monitoring and enforcement mechanisms that would tend to discourage and prevent a new primary landowner from violating federal and state law and/or making rapid or major changes in district operations and services."

In addition, the report catalogues not only the agencies that the District must report to, but also the nearly twenty interlocal governmental agreements that the District had entered into with either Orange or Osceola County. Finally, even though it concludes that sufficient safeguards existed, the report identifies two primary statutory changes that the Legislature could implement to enhance these safeguards. These involved providing further criteria for preventing the District's board members from being replaced by a new owner without cause and placing the District within the state's regional growth management program.

In the end, even though the state legislature was presented with these specific proposals, it chose not to implement either. In fact, it concurred with the OPPAGA's conclusions and did not adopt any statutory amendments to the District's governing authority. This action is significant because if the original experiment of assigning traditional public governance authority to the Reedy Creek "super district" had not achieved stability and success over its thirty-plus years, the state legislature would likely have intervened and ended this unique situation. The failure to do so strongly endorses the overall propriety of the District's regulatory structure.

**Chapter 12** October 1971

# The End of the Beginning

---

Little known to the millions of guests who visit the Walt Disney World Resort each year is the fact that the Reedy Creek Improvement District is the engine that has driven this wildly successful project from a mere idea in Walt Disney's mind to one of the world's largest development projects.

In the process, novel ideas—legal, engineering, legislative, and many others—enabled an effort of unprecedented scope to develop. Indeed, more than providing a regulatory framework for a theme-park resort, the Reedy Creek Improvement District, and Project Future in general, demonstrated that unique allocations of public and private governance can, in appropriate instances, promote visionary efforts.

By the Fall of 1971, Disney's Project Future would begin welcoming millions of guests into its magical world. Yet even the project's opening would yield a final surprise. Despite preparations for throngs of visitors, only ten thousand guests attended the Magic Kingdom's opening on October 1, 1971.

Could all of this work possibly result in a failure? Wall Street's first response was to knock off nearly 10 percent of the company's stock price, while some commentators even wildly predicted the entire resort would close by Thanksgiving.

Perseverance was always one of Project Future's strongest traits, though. Walt Disney's vision was too grand to be felled by early nay-sayers. Indeed, by the following summer, the stock price had rocketed above $175 per share.

The company had also predicted six million guests during the park's first year. Over ten million showed up.

Project Future had once again overcome another potential problem. Today it is one of the world's most visited tourist venues.

## Appendix A

# Key Players and Their Roles in Project Future

---

### Emily Bavar

a reporter with the *Orlando Sentinel-Star*. After attending a press event in Anaheim, California, to discuss Disneyland's tenth anniversary, in October 1965 she reported the "mystery industry" buying land in Florida was Disney. While other reporters had written articles suggesting that Disney might be the mystery land purchaser, Bavar is usually credited as the reporter who first broke the news.

### Irlo Bronson

a Florida State Senator who owned a large tract of land in Osceola County, Florida. In May 1965, Disney purchased 8,380 acres of this land for Project Future from Senator Bronson at the cost of $900,000.

## Haydon Burns

the Governor of Florida who negotiated with Disney in
1965 regarding Disney's decision to locate Project Future
in Florida. Burns made the official announcement of the
project at the Florida League of Municipalities Convention
on Monday, October 25, 1965 following Emily Bavar's
article disclosing Disney as the mystery company buying
large amounts of land in Central Florida. Burns lost re-
election in the 1966 Democratic primary before Disney
introduced its legislative package in the Florida state
legislature.

## Marvin Davis

an art director who designed much of the Disneyland plan.
Walt later tapped him to design the Project Future master
plan, including work on the Magic Kingdom and the
original concept of EPCOT.

## Jack and Bill Demetree

two brothers who sold Disney an option in 1964 for the
surface rights to a twelve thousand-plus acre tract that
composed a significant portion of the Project Future
property. Disney exercised that option in June 1965 after
negotiating with Tufts University for the subsurface rights
to the property. The Demetrees had originally purchased
the parcel in 1959 from Senator Irlo Bronson, who had
purchased the property's surface rights from Tufts
University.

## Tom DeWolf

a Florida attorney who practiced with Paul Helliwell's law firm. DeWolf provided legal and regulatory counsel for the purchase of Project Future parcels and for the development of the Reedy Creek Improvement District. DeWolf was also a long-time Chairman of the Board of Supervisors for the Reedy Creek Improvement District.

## Billy Dial

the Orlando banking executive and business leader whose help and influence kept Disney's identity as the mystery industry secret until the company could complete the purchase of Project Future's vast land holdings. Dial also played a significant role in convincing several hold-out landowners to sell their parcels to Disney-controlled entities.

## Roy O. Disney

Disney's older brother who focused on the company's business interests. After Walt's death in 1966, Roy Disney made the decision to go forward with Project Future.

## Walter Elias "Walt" Disney

the youngest Disney son who was the creative visionary of Disneyland and Project Future, later named Disney World. The theme parks exist because of him.

## Bob Elrod

the well-respected Florida State Senator whom Disney tapped to shepherd its Project Future legislative package through the state legislature. The legislative package

ultimately passed the State House and Senate with only
one vote against it.

### Robert Price Foster

the Disney attorney who had served as legal counsel for
Disneyland. Walt Disney assigned Foster the responsibility
of identifying and acquiring land for Project Future. Foster
also played a significant role in the development, passage,
and implementation of the legislative package for Project
Future.

### Helmut Furth

an attorney at the Donovan, Leisure firm. He served as
Disney's outside legal counsel. Furth drafted much of
the legislation submitted to the Florida legislature. The
legislation ultimately made Project Future a reality.

### Roy Hawkins

a well-connected Florida businessman who provided
political and real estate counsel to Disney during the
identification of land and its acquisition process. Hawkins
worked closely with Robert Foster and Paul Helliwell in
securing most of the Project Future parcels.

### Paul Helliwell

a Florida attorney who served as Disney's lead legal
counsel in Florida during the Project Future process.
In addition to providing legal and regulatory advice,
Helliwell used his extensive business and political
connections to provide valuable strategic advice for the
project.

## Claude Kirk

the Florida Governor who succeeded Haydon Burns and served as governor during the passage of Project Future's legislative package. Kirk signed the actual legislation on May 12, 1967.

## William Lund

the Economic Research Associates official who originally travelled to Florida in late 1963 to begin identifying potential areas and parcels for Project Future. Lund toured the state, including the Orlando area, on behalf of Disney under the strict instructions not to identify his client or negotiate for actual parcels.

## John MacArthur

a colorful South Florida billionaire who had made much of his money by starting the Bankers Life and Casualty Company. MacArthur owned large amounts of property in the Palm Beach area. In the late 1950s, Walt Disney and other company officials travelled to South Florida on different occasions to consider the possibility of building a company project in the area. The company ultimately opted not to build in that part of Florida.

## Harrison "Buzz" Price

the head of Economic Research Associates, the consulting firm Walt Disney hired to provide economic forecasting and other planning services such as initial land identification for Project Future. Disney had previously hired Price to provide similar services for Disneyland and other proposed Disney projects.

## Joe Potter

a former executive with the 1964-1965 New York World's Fair. Disney hired him to manage the development and construction of Project Future. Potter would later serve as Chairman of the Board of Supervisors for the Reedy Creek Improvement District.

## Card Walker

the Disney executive who originally supported building Disney's eastern U.S. project in St. Louis or the eastern seaboard as opposed to Florida. He later became both Chairman and CEO of Disney during the time the company opened the EPCOT theme park.

# The Project Future Timeline

## July 1955
Disneyland opens.

## December 1959
Walt Disney explores the possibility of building a new entertainment project in Palm Beach County, Florida on land owned by billionaire John MacArthur.

## March 1963
Walt Disney begins discussions with St. Louis officials about developing a new entertainment project on the city's waterfront.

## August 1963
Walt Disney tours several locations in the eastern United States as prospective sites for a new entertainment project.

These locations included Niagara Falls and New York
City, the site of the 1964-65 World's Fair where Disney was
developing several projects.

## November 1963
Walt Disney and other Disney executives make their first
visit to the area of Central Florida that would ultimately
become the location of Project Future. During the visit, the
group toured sites in the City of Ocala, Osceola County,
and Orange County, Florida.

## January 1964
Economic Research Associates completes a study on
available land in Florida for Project Future.

## February/March 1964
Disney lawyer Robert Foster travels to Florida to meet with
Miami attorney Paul Helliwell about representing Disney's
interests in Florida. Disney subsequently hires Helliwell's
law firm.

## April 1964
Disney hires Roy Hawkins to advise the company in
identifying and purchasing land in Florida for Project
Future.

## May 1964
Robert Foster, Paul Helliwell, and Roy Hawkins begin
to focus on several parcels in Central Florida for Project
Future. Later that month, Foster tours the Demetree Tract,
a parcel that would eventually become the centerpiece of
Project Future.

## June 1964

Disney obtains an option for the Demetree parcel.

## August 1964

Disney obtains an option for another significant parcel of Project Future, the Bay Lake tract.

## September 1964

Disney obtains an option for a third major parcel of Project Future, the Hamrick tract.

## May 1965

Disney purchases an 8,000 + acre parcel in Osceola County, Florida from State Senator Irlo Bronson. This parcel was Disney's first major land purchase for Project Future.

## May/June 1965

Disney completes the purchase of the Demetree, Bay Lake, and Hamrick parcels.

## June 1965

Disney officials gather with outside advisors for a meeting in Burbank at which the company finalizes its decision to build Project Future.

## October 1, 1965

Helliwell announces that the mystery company will reveal its identity at a November 15th press conference.

## October 17, 1965

The *Orlando Star-Sentinel* publishes an article by Emily Bavar claiming that Disney is the mystery company.

## October 25, 1965

With Disney officials in the audience, Governor Haydon Burns announces during a speech at Florida League of Municipalities Convention that Disney is the mystery company coming to Central Florida.

## November 15, 1965

Walt Disney, Roy Disney, and Governor Haydon Burns gather at the Cherry Plaza Hotel in Orlando where they meet with business leaders and the press to provide details related to Project Future.

## June 1966

Marvin Davis, the Disney official who designed much of the master plan for Disneyland, begins designs for Project Future.

## December 1966

Walt Disney passes away.

## April 1967

Disney introduces the Project Future legislative package before the State House and State Senate.

## May 12, 1967

After receiving near unanimous approval in the State Legislature, Governor Claude Kirk signs the Project Future legislative package into law at a ceremony attended by Roy Disney.

## November 1968

The Florida Supreme Court upholds the validity of the legislative package for Project Future.

**April 1969**

Disney holds a large event for business leaders and members of the press to announce additional details related to Project Future

**October 1971**

Project Future opens.

# Bibliography

---

Writing this book required a great deal of research from a wide variety of sources.  In this section, I have tried to highlight some key examples of these sources.  This is not intended as an exhaustive list because there are so many different books and other resources on the topic of Walt Disney and his career and projects.  Instead, these sources provide a good place to begin research into how Disney ended up in Central Florida.

## Books

Bob Thomas, <u>Building a Company:  Roy O. Disney and the Creation of an Entertainment Empire</u> (1998).

Frances Novak-Branch, The Disney World Effect (1983).

Jason Surrell, <u>The Disney Mountains:  Imagineering at Its Peak</u> (2007).

Richard E. Foglesong, <u>Married to the Mouse</u> (2001).

Steve Manheim, <u>Walt Disney and the Quest for Community</u> (2002).

## Articles

Alecia Swasy, *Off the Shelf; When Disney Winked, Florida Swooned*, N.Y. TIMES, July 8, 2001.

*Disney Dollars*, FORBES MAG., May 1, 1971.

*Disneyworld Amusement Center with Domed City Set for Florida*, N.Y. TIMES, Feb. 3, 1967.

*Disney World Triggers Trouble for Orlando*, BUS. WK., Apr. 1, 1972.

*Disney World Wakes Sleepy Orlando*, BUS. WK., Nov. 14, 1970.

Elliot McCleary, *Will 10,000,000 People Ruin All This?*, NAT'L WILDLIFE, June-July 1971.

Jon Nordheimer, *New Disney World Is Rising*, N.Y. TIMES, Dec. 29, 1970.

*Land Speculators Play Disney's Money Machine*, BUS. WK., Sept. 11, 1971.

Robert N. Jenkins, *How One Man, and One Mouse, Changed Us*, St. Petersburg Times, Dec. 12, 1999.

*Study: Disney Still Drives C. Fla. Economy*, Orlando Bus. J., May 28, 2004.

William W. Buzbee, *Accountability Conceptions and Federalism Tales: Disney's Wonderful World?*, 100 Mich. L. Rev. 1290 (2002).

## Government Materials

### Federal
A.L. Putnam, U.S. Geological Surv., Summary of Hydrologic Conditions and Effects of the Walt Disney World Development in the Reedy Creek Improvement District, 1966-73 (1975).

File of the Florida Ranchlands lawsuit against Disney in the National Archives, Southeast Branch.

### State
Office of Program Policy Analysis and Gov't Accountability, Fla. Leg., Central Florida's Reedy Creek Improvement District Has Wide-Ranging Authority, Rep. No. 04-81 (2004).

E. Cent. Fla. Reg'l Planning Council, Key Findings 1965 Research Series (1965).

<u>Local</u>

Minutes of the Board of Supervisors of Reedy Creek
        Drainage District

## **Interviews and Special Collections**

Economics    Research    Associates,    Preliminary
Investigation of Available Acreage for Project Winter (Jan.
16, 1964) (unpublished report, on file with the Special
Collections and University Archives, University of Central
Florida).

Economics Research Associates, Summary of Disney-
Oriented Projects (Oct. 18, 1963) (on file with the Special
Collections and University Archives, University of Central
Florida).

Inter-Office    Communication    from    Jack    Sayers    to
Florida Committee 1 (June 6, 1966) (on file with the Special
Collections and University Archives, University of Central
Florida).

Interview with Thomas DeWolf (Aug. 8, 2007).

Summary of Project Future Seminar (on file with the
Special Collections and University Archives, University of
Central Florida).

# Notes

---

[1] The account of the Goldstein matter was well-described by Richard Fogelsong in his book, <u>Married to the Mouse</u>.

[2] Billy Dial recollected on his conversation with Roy Disney during an interview with the Florida Oral History Program in September 1987.

[3] *State v. Reedy Creek Improvement District*, 216 So.2d 202 (Fla. 1968).

[4] The story of the FRL discovery of Fowler's identity was well told by Richard Fogelsong in his book, <u>Married to the Mouse.</u>

[5] Though Disney commissioned the Fishkind study, the study's finding were based on public data and statistics.